Ere Fate had left thee-all alone!

IV.

Thy russet coat is scant, and torn,
Thy cheek is now grown deathly pale!
Thy eyes are dim, thy looks forlorn,
And bare thy bosom meets the gale;
And oft I hear thee deeply groan,
That thou, poor boy, art left alone.

V.

Thy naked feet are wounded sore
With thorns, that cross thy daily road;
The winter winds around thee roar,
The church-yard is thy bleak abode;
Thy pillow now, a cold grave stone—
And there thou lov'st to grieve—alone!

VI.

The rain has drench'd thee, all night long;
The nipping frost thy bosom froze;
And still, the yewtree—shades among,
I heard thee sigh thy artless woes;
I heard thee, till the day-star shone
In darkness weep-and weep alone!

VII.

Oft have I seen thee, little boy,
Upon thy lovely mother's knee;
For when she liv'd—thou wert her joy,
Though now a mourner thou must be!
For she lies low, where yon grave-stone
Proclaims, that thou art left alone.

VIII.

Weep, weep no more; on yonder hill
The village bells are ringing, gay;
The merry reed, and brawling rill

Call thee to rustic sports away.
Then wherefore weep, and sigh, and moan,
A truant from the throng—alone?

IX.

"I cannot the green hill ascend,
"I cannot pace the upland mead;
"I cannot in the vale attend,
"To hear the merry-sounding reed:
"For all is still, beneath yon stone,
"Where my poor mother's left alone!

X.

"I cannot gather gaudy flowers
"To dress the scene of revels loud-
"I cannot pass the ev'ning hours
"Among the noisy village croud—
"For, all in darkness, and alone
"My mother sleeps, beneath yon stone.

XI.

"See how the stars begin to gleam
"The sheep-dog barks, 'tis time to go;—
"The night-fly hums, the moonlight beam
"Peeps through the yew-tree's shadowy row—
"It falls upon the white grave-stone,
"Where my dear mother sleeps alone.—

XII.

"O stay me not, for I must go
"The upland path in haste to tread;
"For there the pale primroses grow
"They grow to dress my mother's bed.—
"They must, ere peep of day, be strown,
"Where she lies mould'ring all alone.

XIII.

"My father o'er the stormy sea

Lyrical Tales by Mary Robinson

Mary Robinson was born in Bristol, England on 27th November 1757.

Her father, Nicholas Darby, a naval captain, deserted her mother, Hester, for his mistress when Mary was still a child. Without the support of her husband, Hester Darby supported her five children by opening a school for young girls in Little Chelsea, London, (where Mary was teaching by her 14th birthday). On a short return to the family, Captain Darby had the school closed which under English law he was entitled to do.

Mary, who at one point attended a school run by the social reformer and poet Hannah More, came to the attention of actor David Garrick. Acting was to her way into the arts, although in those times it was also a chaotic and difficult time for any actress.

A marriage at 15 to a clerk who claimed a large inheritance proved troublesome. After the marriage Mary discovered that her husband had no inheritance but he did have a taste for living way beyond his means and for multiple affairs that he made no effort to hide. Her husband though was now arrested and imprisoned for debt in Fleet Prison. Mary and their six-month old child accompanied him.

However it was here that she discovered she could publish poetry and earn money, as well as be distracted from the harsh reality around her. The result was 'Poems by Mrs. Robinson', published in 1775.

After their release from prison Mary returned to the theatre. Her first performance was playing Juliet, at Drury Lane Theatre in December 1776. Playing Perdita 'A Winter's Tale' at 21 in 1779 attracted the attention of the young Prince of Wales and the offer of twenty thousand pounds to become his mistress.

However, the Prince ended the affair in 1781 and refused to pay the promised sum.

From the late 1780s, Mary's poetry distinguished her so much that she was referred to as 'the English Sappho'. In addition she authored eight novels, three plays, feminist treatises, and an autobiographical manuscript that was incomplete at the time of her death.

Mary Darby Robinson died in poverty at Englefield Cottage, Englefield Green, Surrey, on 26th December 1800, aged 44, having survived several years of ill health.

Index of Contents

ALL ALONE

I.

Ah! wherefore by the Church-yard side,
Poor little LORN ONE, dost thou stray?
Thy wavy locks but thinly hide
The tears that dim thy blue-eye's ray;
And wherefore dost thou sigh, and moan,
And weep, that thou art left alone?

II.

Thou art not left alone, poor boy,
The Trav'ller stops to hear thy tale;
No heart, so hard, would thee annoy!
For tho' thy mother's cheek is pale
And withers under yon grave stone,
Thou art not, Urchin, left alone.

III.

I know thee well! thy yellow hair
In silky waves I oft have seen;
Thy dimpled face, so fresh and fair,
Thy roguish smile, thy playful mien
Were all to me, poor Orphan, known,

"To distant lands was borne away,
"And still my mother stay'd with me
"And wept by night and toil'd by day.
"And shall I ever quit the stone
"Where she is, left, to sleep alone.

XIV.

"My father died; and still I found
"My mother fond and kind to me;
"I felt her breast with rapture bound
"When first I prattled on her knee—
"And then she blest my infant tone
"And little thought of yon grave-stone.

XV.

"No more her gentle voice I hear,
"No more her smile of fondness see;
"Then wonder not I shed the tear
"She would have DIED, to follow me!
"And yet she sleeps beneath yon stone
"And I STILL LIVE—to weep alone.

XVI.

"The playful kid, she lov'd so well
"From yon high clift was seen to fall;
"I heard, afar, his tink'ling bell—
"Which seem'd in vain for aid to call—
"I heard the harmless suff'rer moan,
"And grieved that he was left alone.

XVII.

"Our faithful dog grew mad, and died,
"The lightning smote our cottage low—
"We had no resting-place beside
"And knew not whither we should go,—
"For we were poor,—and hearts of stone
"Will never throb at mis'ry's groan.

XVIII.

"My mother still surviv'd for me,
"She led me to the mountain's brow,
"She watch'd me, while at yonder tree
"I sat, and wove the ozier bough;
"And oft she cried, "fear not, MINE OWN!
"Thou shalt not, BOY, be left ALONE."

XIX.

"The blast blew strong, the torrent rose
"And bore our shatter'd cot away;
"And, where the clear brook swiftly flows—
"Upon the turf at dawn of day,
"When bright the sun's full lustre shone,
"I wander'd, FRIENDLESS—and ALONE!"

XX.

Thou art not, boy, for I have seen
Thy tiny footsteps print the dew,
And while the morning sky serene
Spread o'er the hill a yellow hue,
I heard thy sad and plaintive moan,
Beside the cold sepulchral stone.

XXI.

And when the summer noontide hours
With scorching rays the landscape spread,
I mark'd thee, weaving fragrant flow'rs
To deck thy mother's silent bed!
Nor, at the church-yard's simple stone,
Wert, thou, poor Urchin, left alone.

XXII.

I follow'd thee, along the dale
And up the woodland's shad'wy way:
I heard thee tell thy mournful tale
As slowly sunk the star of day:
Nor, when its twinkling light had flown,
Wert thou a wand'rer, all alone.

XXIII.

"O! yes, I was! and still shall be
"A wand'rer, mourning and forlorn;
"For what is all the world to me—
"What are the dews and buds of morn?
"Since she, who left me sad, alone
"In darkness sleeps, beneath yon stone!

XXIV.

"No brother's tear shall fall for me,
"For I no brother ever knew;
"No friend shall weep my destiny
"For friends are scarce, and tears are few;
"None do I see, save on this stone
"Where I will stay, and weep alone!

XXV.

"My Father never will return,
"He rests beneath the sea-green wave;
"I have no kindred left, to mourn
"When I am hid in yonder grave!
"Not one! to dress with flow'rs the stone;—
"Then-surely, I AM LEFT ALONE!"

THE MISTLETOE

A CHRISTMAS TALE

A farmer's wife, both young and gay,
And fresh as op'ning buds of May;
Had taken to herself, a Spouse,
And plighted many solemn vows,
That she a faithful mate would prove,
In meekness, duty, and in love!
That she, despising Joy and wealth,
Would be, in sickness and in health,
His only comfort and his Friend-
But, mark the sequel,—and attend!
This Farmer, as the tale is told—
Was somewhat cross, and somewhat old!

His, was the wintry hour of life,
While summer smiled before his wife;
A contrast, rather form'd to cloy
The zest of matrimonial joy!
'Twas Christmas time, the peasant throng
Assembled gay, with dance and Song:
The Farmer's Kitchen long had been
Of annual sports the busy scene;
The wood-fire blaz'd, the chimney wide
Presented seats, on either side;
Long rows of wooden Trenchers, clean,
Bedeck'd with holly-boughs, were seen;
The shining Tankard's foamy ale
Gave spirits to the Goblin tale,
And many a rosy cheek—grew pale.
It happen'd, that some sport to shew
The ceiling held a MISTLETOE.
A magic bough, and well design'd
To prove the coyest Maiden, kind.

A magic bough, which DRUIDS old
Its sacred mysteries enroll'd;
And which, or gossip Fame's a liar,
Still warms the soul with vivid fire;
Still promises a store of bliss
While bigots snatch their Idol's kiss.
This MISTLETOE was doom'd to be
The talisman of Destiny;
Beneath its ample boughs we're told
Full many a timid Swain grew bold;
Full many a roguish eye askance
Beheld it with impatient glance,
And many a ruddy cheek confest,
The triumphs of the beating breast;
And many a rustic rover sigh'd
Who ask'd the kiss, and was denied.
First MARG'RY smil'd and gave her Lover
A Kiss; then thank'd her stars, 'twas over!

Next, KATE, with a reluctant pace,
Was tempted to the mystic place;
Then SUE, a merry laughing jade
A dimpled yielding blush betray'd;
While JOAN her chastity to shew
Wish'd "the bold knaves would serve her so,"
She'd "teach the rogues such wanton play!"
And well she could, she knew the way.

The FARMER, mute with jealous care,
Sat sullen, in his wicker chair;
Hating the noisy gamesome host
Yet, fearful to resign his post;
He envied all their sportive strife
But most he watch'd his blooming wife,
And trembled, lest her steps should go,
Incautious, near the MISTLETOE.
Now HODGE, a youth of rustic grace
With form athletic; manly face;

On MISTRESS HOMESPUN turn'd his eye
And breath'd a soul-declaring sigh!
Old HOMESPUN, mark'd his list'ning Fair
And nestled in his wicker chair;
HODGE swore, she might his heart command-
The pipe was dropp'd from HOMESPUN'S hand!
HODGE prest her slender waist around;
The FARMER check'd his draught, and frown'd!
And now beneath the MISTLETOE
'Twas MISTRESS HOMESPUN'S turn to go;
Old Surly shook his wicker chair,
And sternly utter'd—"Let her dare!"
HODGE, to the FARMER'S wife declar'd
Such husbands never should be spar'd;
Swore, they deserv'd the worst disgrace,
That lights upon the wedded race;
And vow'd-that night he would not go
Unblest, beneath the MISTLETOE.

The merry group all recommend
An harmless Kiss, the strife to end:
"Why not?" says MARG'RY, "who would fear,
"A dang'rous moment, once a year?"
SUSAN observ'd, that "ancient folks
"Were seldom pleas'd with youthful jokes;"
But KATE, who, till that fatal hour,
Had held, o'er HODGE, unrivall'd pow'r,
With curving lip and head aside
Look'd down and smil'd in conscious pride,
Then, anxious to conceal her care,
She humm'd-"what fools some women are!"
Now, MISTRESS HOMESPUN, sorely vex'd,
By pride and jealous rage perplex'd,
And angry, that her peevish spouse
Should doubt her matrimonial vows,
But, most of all, resolved to make
An envious rival's bosom ache;

Commanded Hodge to let her go,
Nor lead her to the Mistletoe;

"Why should you ask it o'er and o'er?"
Cried she, "we've been there twice before!"
'Tis thus, to check a rival's sway,
That Women oft themselves betray;
While VANITY, alone, pursuing,
They rashly prove, their own undoing.

THE POOR, SINGING DAME

Beneath an old wall, that went round an old Castle,
For many a year, with brown ivy o'erspread;
A neat little Hovel, its lowly roof raising,
Defied the wild winds that howl'd over its shed:
The turrets, that frown'd on the poor simple dwelling,
Were rock'd to and fro, when the Tempest would roar,
And the river, that down the rich valley was swelling,
Flow'd swiftly beside the green step of its door.

The Summer Sun, gilded the rushy-roof slanting,
The bright dews bespangled its ivy-bound hedge
And above, on the ramparts, the sweet Birds were chanting,
And wild buds thick dappled the clear river's edge.
When the Castle's rich chambers were haunted, and dreary,
The poor little Hovel was still, and secure;
And no robber e'er enter'd, or goblin or fairy,
For the splendours of pride had no charms to allure.

The Lord of the Castle, a proud, surly ruler,
Oft heard the low dwelling with sweet music ring:
For the old Dame that liv'd in the little Hut chearly,
Would sit at her wheel, and would merrily sing:
When with revels the Castle's great Hall was resounding,
The Old Dame was sleeping, not dreaming of fear;
And when over the mountains the Huntsmen were bounding
She would open her wicket, their clamours to hear.

To the merry-ton'd horn, she would dance on the threshold,
And louder, and louder, repeat her old Song:
And when Winter its mantle of Frost was displaying
She caroll'd, undaunted, the bare woods among:
She would gather dry Fern, ever happy and singing,
With her cake of brown bread, and her jug of brown beer,
And would smile when she heard the great Castle-bell ringing,

Inviting the Proud—to their prodigal chear.

Thus she liv'd, ever patient and ever contented,
Till Envy the Lord of the Castle possess'd,
For he hated that Poverty should be so chearful,
While care could the fav'rites of Fortune molest;
He sent his bold yeomen with threats to prevent her,
And still would she carol her sweet roundelay;
At last, an old Steward, relentless he sent her—
Who bore her, all trembling, to Prison away!

Three weeks did she languish, then died, broken-hearted,
Poor Dame! how the death-bell did mournfully sound!
And along the green path six young Bachelors bore her,
And laid her, for ever, beneath the cold ground!
And the primroses pale, 'mid the long grass were growing,
The bright dews of twilight bespangled her grave
And morn heard the breezes of summer soft blowing
To bid the fresh flow'rets in sympathy wave.

The Lord of the Castle, from that fatal moment
When poor Singing MARY was laid in her grave,
Each night was surrounded by Screech-owls appalling,
Which o'er the black turrets their pinions would wave!
On the ramparts that frown'd on the river, swift flowing,
They hover'd, still hooting a terrible song,
When his windows would rattle, the Winter blast blowing,
They would shriek like a ghost, the dark alleys among!

Wherever he wander'd they followed him crying,
At dawnlight, at Eve, still they haunted his way!
When the Moon shone across the wide common, they hooted,
Nor quitted his path, till the blazing of day.
His bones began wasting, his flesh was decaying,
And he hung his proud head, and he perish'd with shame;
And the tomb of rich marble, no soft tear displaying,
O'ershadows the grave, of THE POOR SINGING DAME!

MISTRESS GURTON'S CAT

A DOMESTIC TALE

Old MISTRESS GURTON had a Cat,
A Tabby, loveliest of the race,
Sleek as a doe, and tame, and fat
With velvet paws, and whisker'd face;

The Doves of VENUS not so fair,
Nor JUNO'S Peacocks half so grand
As MISTRESS GURTON'S Tabby rare,
The proudest of the purring band;
So dignified in all her paces—
She seem'd, a pupil of the Graces!
There never was a finer creature
In all the varying whims of Nature!

All liked Grimalkin, passing well!
Save MISTRESS GURTON, and, 'tis said,
She oft with furious ire would swell,
When, through neglect or hunger keen,
Puss, with a pilfer'd scrap, was seen,
Swearing beneath the pent-house shed:
For, like some fav'rites, she was bent
On all things, yet with none content;
And still, whate'er her place or diet,
She could not pick her bone, in quiet.
Sometimes, new milk GRIMALKIN stole,
And sometimes-over-set the bowl!
For over eagerness will prove,
Oft times the bane of what we love;
And sometimes, to her neighbour's home,
GRIMALKIN, like a thief would roam,
Teaching poor Cats, of humbler kind,
For high example sways the mind!
Sometimes she paced the garden wall,
Thick guarded by the shatter'd pane,
And lightly treading with disdain,
Fear'd not Ambition's certain fall!
Old China broke, or scratch'd her Dame
And brought domestic friends to shame!
And many a time this Cat was curst,
Of squalling, thieving things, the worst!
Wish'd Dead! and menac'd with a string,
For Cats of such scant Fame, deserv'd to swing!
One day, report, for ever busy,
Resolv'd to make Dame Gurton easy;
A Neighbour came, with solemn look,
And thus, the dismal tidings broke.
"Know you, that poor GRIMALKIN died
"Last night, upon the pent-house side?
"I heard her for assistance call;
"I heard her shrill and dying squall!
"I heard her, in reproachful tone,
"Pour, to the stars, her feeble groan!

"Alone, I heard her piercing cries—
"With not a Friend to close her Eyes!"
"Poor Puss! I vow it grieves me sore,
"Never to see thy beauties more!
"Never again to hear thee purr,
"To stroke thy back, of Zebra fur;
"To see thy emral'd eyes—so bright,
"Flashing around their lust'rous light
"Amid the solemn shades of night!
"Methinks I see her pretty paws—
"As gracefully she paced along;
"I hear her voice, so shrill, among
"The chimney rows! I see her claws,
"While, like a Tyger, she pursued
"Undauntedly the pilf'ring race;
"I see her lovely whisker'd face
"When she her nimble prey subdued!
"And then, how she would frisk, and play,
"And purr the Evening hours away:

"Now stretch'd beside the social fire;
"Now on the sunny lawn, at noon,
"Watching the vagrant Birds that flew,
"Across the scene of varied hue,
"To peck the Fruit. Or when the Moon
"Stole o'er the hills, in silv'ry suit,
"How would she chaunt her lovelorn Tale
"Soft as the wild Eolian Lyre!
"'Till ev'ry brute, on hill, in dale,
"Listen'd with wonder mute!"
"O! Cease!" exclaim'd DAME GURTON, straight,
"Has my poor Puss been torn away?
"Alas! how cruel is my fate,
"How shall I pass the tedious day?
"Where can her mourning mistress find
"So sweet a Cat? so meek! so kind!
"So keen a mouser, such a beauty,
"So orderly, so fond, so true,
"That every gentle task of duty
"The dear, domestic creature knew!
"Hers, was the mildest tend'rest heart!
"She knew no little cattish art;
"Not cross, like fav'rite Cats, was she
"But seem'd the queen of Cats to be!
"I cannot live-since doom'd, alas! to part
"From poor GRIMALKIN kind, the darling of my heart!"
And now DAME GURTON, bath'd in tears,
With a black top-knot vast, appears:

Some say that a black gown she wore,
As many oft have done before,
For Beings, valued less, I ween,
Than this, of Tabby Cats, the fav'rite Queen!
But lo! soon after, one fair day,
Puss, who had only been a roving—
Across the pent-house took her way,
To see her Dame, so sad, and loving;
Eager to greet the mourning fair
She enter'd by a window, where
A China bowl of luscious cream
Was quiv'ring in the sunny beam.
Puss, who was somewhat tired and dry,
And somewhat fond of bev'rage sweet;
Beholding such a tempting treat,
Resolved its depth to try.
She saw the warm and dazzling ray
Upon the spotless surface play:
She purr'd around its circle wide,
And gazed, and long'd, and mew'd and sigh'd!
But Fate, unfriendly, did that hour controul,
She overset the cream, and smash'd the gilded bowl!
As MISTRESS GURTON heard the thief,
She started from her easy chair,
And, quite unmindful of her grief,
Began aloud to swear!
"Curse that voracious beast!" she cried,
"Here SUSAN bring a cord—

"I'll hang the vicious, ugly creature—
"The veriest plague e'er form'd by nature!"
And MISTRESS GURTON kept her word-
And Poor GRIMALKIN—DIED!
Thus, often, we with anguish sore
The dead, in clam'rous grief deplore;
Who, were they once alive again
Would meet the sting of cold disdain!
For FRIENDS, whom trifling faults can sever,
Are valued most, WHEN LOST FOR EVER!

THE LASCAR

IN TWO PARTS

I.

"Another day, Ah! me, a day
"Of dreary Sorrow is begun!
"And still I loath the temper'd ray,
"And still I hate the sickly Sun!
"Far from my Native Indian shore,
"I hear our wretched race deplore;
"I mark the smile of taunting Scorn,
"And curse the hour, when I was born!
"I weep, but no one gently tries
"To stop my tear, or check my sighs;
"For, while my heart beats mournfully,
"Dear Indian home, I sigh for Thee!

II.

"Since, gaudy Sun! I see no more
"Thy hottest glory gild the day;
"Since, sever'd from my burning shore,
"I waste the vapid hours away;
"O! darkness come! come, deepest gloom!
"Shroud the young Summer's op'ning bloom;
"Burn, temper'd Orb, with fiercer beams
"This northern world! and drink the streams
"That thro' the fertile vallies glide
"To bathe the feasted Fiends of Pride!
"Or, hence, broad Sun! extinguish'd be!
"For endless night encircles Me!

III.

"What is, to me, the City gay?
"And what, the board profusely spread?
"I have no home, no rich array,
"No spicy feast, no downy bed!
"I, with the dogs am doom'd to eat,
"To perish in the peopled street,
"To drink the tear of deep despair;
"The scoff and scorn of fools to bear!
"I sleep upon a bed of stone,
"I pace the meadows, wild alone!
"And if I curse my fate severe,
"Some Christian Savage mocks my tear!

IV.

"Shut out the Sun, O! pitying Night!
"Make the wide world my silent tomb!
"O'ershade this northern, sickly light,
"And shroud me, in eternal gloom!
"My Indian plains, now smiling glow,
"There stands my Parent's hovel low,
"And there the tow'ring aloes rise
"And fling their perfumes to the skies!
"There the broad palm Trees covert lend,
"There Sun and Shade delicious blend;
"But here, amid the blunted ray,
"Cold shadows hourly cross my way!

V.

"Was it for this, that on the main
"I met the tempest fierce and strong,
"And steering o'er the liquid plain,
"Still onward, press'd the waves among?
"Was it for this, the LASCAR brave
"Toil'd, like a wretched Indian Slave;
"Preserv'd your treasures by his toil,
"And sigh'd to greet this fertile soil?
"Was it for this, to beg, to die,
"Where plenty smiles, and where the Sky
"Sheds cooling airs; while fev'rish pain,
"Maddens the famish'd LASCAR'S brain?

VI.

"Oft, I the stately Camel led,
"And sung the short-hour'd night away;
"And oft, upon the top-mast's head,
"Hail'd the red Eye of coming day.
"The Tanyan's back my mother bore;
"And oft the wavy Ganges' roar
"Lull'd her to rest, as on she past—
"'Mid the hot sands and burning blast!
"And oft beneath the Banyan tree
"She sate and fondly nourish'd me;
"And while the noontide hour past slow,
"I felt her breast with kindness glow.

VII.

"Where'er I turn my sleepless eyes,

"No cheek so dark as mine, I see;
"For Europe's Suns, with softer dyes
"Mark Europe's favour'd progeny!
"Low is my stature, black my hair,
"The emblem of my Soul's despair!
"My voice no dulcet cadence flings,
"To touch soft pity's throbbing strings!
"Then wherefore cruel Briton, say,
"Compel my aching heart to stay?
"To-morrow's Sun—may rise, to see—
"The famish'd LASCAR, blest as thee!"

VIII.

The morn had scarcely shed its rays
When, from the City's din he ran;
For he had fasted, four long days,
And faint his Pilgrimage began!
The LASCAR, now, without a friend,—
Up the steep hill did slow ascend;
Now o'er the flow'ry meadows stole,
While pain, and hunger, pinch'd his Soul;
And now his fev'rish lip was dried,
And burning tears his thirst supply'd,
And, ere he saw the Ev'ning close,
Far off, the City dimly rose!

IX.

Again the Summer Sun flam'd high
The plains were golden, far and wide;
And fervid was the cloudless sky,
And slow the breezes seem'd to glide:
The gossamer, on briar and spray,
Shone silv'ry in the solar ray;
And sparkling dew-drops, falling round
Spangled the hot and thirsty ground;
The insect myriads humm'd their tune
To greet the coming hour of noon,
While the poor LASCAR Boy, in haste,
Flew, frantic, o'er the sultry waste

X.

And whither could the wand'rer go?

Who would receive a stranger poor?
Who, when the blasts of night should blow,
Would ope to him the friendly door?
Alone, amid the race of man,
The sad, the fearful alien ran!
None would an Indian wand'rer bless;
None greet him with the fond caress;
None feed him, though with hunger keen
He at the Lordly gate were seen,
Prostrate, and humbly forc'd to crave
A shelter, for an Indian Slave.

XI.

The noon-tide Sun, now flaming wide,
No cloud its fierce beam shadow'd o'er,
But what could worse to him betide
Than begging, at the proud man's door?
For clos'd and lofty was the gate,
And there, in all the pride of State,
A surly Porter turn'd the key,
A man of sullen soul was he—
His brow was fair; but in his eye
Sat pamper'd scorn, and tyranny;
And, near him, a fierce mastiff stood,
Eager to bathe his fangs in blood.

XII.

The weary LASCAR turn'd away,
For trembling fear his heart subdued,
And down his cheek the tear would stray,
Though burning anguish drank his blood!
The angry Mastiff snarl'd, as he
Turn'd from the house of luxury;
The sultry hour was long, and high
The broad-sun flamed athwart the sky—
But still a throbbing hope possess'd
The Indian wand'rer's fev'rish breast,
When from the distant dell a sound
Of swelling music echo'd round.

XIII.

It was the church-bell's merry peal;

And now a pleasant house he view'd:
And now his heart began to feel
As though, it were not quite subdu'd!
No lofty dome, shew'd loftier state,
No pamper'd Porter watch'd the gate,
No Mastiff, like a tyrant stood,
Eager to scatter human blood;
Yet the poor Indian wand'rer found,
E'en where Religion smil'd around—
That tears had little pow'r to speak
When trembling, on a sable cheek!

XIV.

With keen reproach, and menace rude,
The LASCAR Boy away was sent;
And now again he seem'd subdu'd,
And his soul sicken'd, as he went.
Now, on the river's bank he stood;
Now, drank the cool refreshing flood;
Again his fainting heart beat high;
Again he rais'd his languid eye;
Then, from the upland's sultry side,
Look'd back, forgave the wretch, and sigh'd!
While the proud PASTOR bent his way
To preach of CHARITY-and PRAY!

PART SECOND

I.

The LASCAR Boy still journey'd on,
For the hot Sun, HE well could bear,
And now the burning hour was gone,
And Evening came, with softer air!
The breezes kiss'd his sable breast,
While his scorch'd feet the cold dew prest;
The waving flow'rs soft tears display'd,
And songs of rapture fill'd the glade,
The South-wind quiver'd, o'er the stream
Reflecting back the rosy beam,
While, as the purpling twilight clos'd,
On a turf bed-the Boy repos'd!

II.

And now, in fancy's airy dream,
The LASCAR Boy his Mother spied;
And, from her breast, a crimson stream
Slow trickled down her beating side:
And now he heard her wild, complain,
As loud she shriek'd-but shriek'd in vain!
And now she sunk upon the ground,
The red stream trickling from her wound,
And near her feet a murd'rer stood,
His glitt'ring poniard tipp'd with blood!
And now, "farewell, my son!" she cried,
Then clos'd her fainting eyes—and died!

III.

The Indian Wand'rer, waking, gaz'd
With grief, and pain, and horror wild;
And tho' his fev'rish brain was craz'd,
He rais'd his eyes to Heav'n, and smil'd!
And now the stars were twinkling clear,
And the blind Bat was whirling near;
And the lone Owlet shriek'd, while He
Still sate beneath a shelt'ring tree;
And now the fierce-ton'd midnight blast
Across the wide heath, howling past,
When a long cavalcade he spied
By torch-light near the river's side.

IV.

He rose, and hast'ning swiftly on,
Call'd loudly to the Sumptuous train,—
But soon the cavalcade was gone-
And darkness wrapp'd the scene again.
He follow'd still the distant sound;
He saw the lightning flashing round;
He heard the crashing thunder roar;
He felt the whelming torrents pour;
And, now beneath a shelt'ring wood
He listen'd to the tumbling flood—
And now, with falt'ring, feeble breath,
The famish'd LASCAR, pray'd for Death.

V.

And now the flood began to rise
And foaming rush'd along the vale;
The LASCAR watch'd, with stedfast eyes,
The flash descending quick and pale;
And now again the cavalcade
Pass'd slowly near the upland glade;—
But HE was dark, and dark the scene,
The torches long extinct had been;
He call'd, but, in the stormy hour,
His feeble voice had lost its pow'r,
'Till, near a tree, beside the flood,
A night-bewilder'd Trav'ller stood.

VI.

The LASCAR now with transport ran
"Stop! stop!" he cried-with accents bold;
The Trav'ller was a fearful man—
And next his life he priz'd his gold!—
He heard the wand'rer madly cry;
He heard his footsteps following nigh;
He nothing saw, while onward prest,
Black as the sky, the Indian's breast;
Till his firm grasp he felt, while cold
Down his pale cheek the big drop roll'd;
Then, struggling to be free, he gave—
A deep wound to the LASCAR Slave.

VII.

And now he groan'd, by pain opprest,
And now crept onward, sad and slow:
And while he held his bleeding breast,
He feebly pour'd the plaint of woe!
"What have I done?" the LASCAR cried—
"That Heaven to me the pow'r denied
"To touch the soul of man, and share
"A brother's love, a brother's care;
"Why is this dingy form decreed
"To bear oppression's scourge and bleed?—
"Is there a GOD, in yon dark Heav'n,
"And shall such monsters be forgiv'n?

VIII.

"Here, in this smiling land we find
"Neglect and mis'ry sting our race;
"And still, whate'er the LASCAR'S mind,
"The stamp of sorrow marks his face!"
He ceas'd to speak; while from his side
Fast roll'd life's swiftly-ebbing tide,
And now, though sick and faint was he,
He slowly climb'd a tall Elm tree,
To watch, if, near his lonely way,
Some friendly Cottage lent a ray,
A little ray of chearful light,
To gild the LASCAR'S long, long night!

IX.

And now he hears a distant bell,
His heart is almost rent with joy!
And who, but such a wretch can tell,
The transports of the Indian boy?
And higher now he climbs the tree,
And hopes some shelt'ring Cot to see;
Again he listens, while the peal
Seems up the woodland vale to steal;
The twinkling stars begin to fade,
And dawnlight purples o'er the glade—
And while the sev'ring vapours flee,
The LASCAR boy looks chearfully!

X.

And now the Sun begins to rise
Above the Eastern summit blue;
And o'er the plain the day-breeze flies,
And sweetly bloom the fields of dew!
The wand'ring wretch was chill'd, for he
Sate, shiv'ring in the tall Elm tree;
And he was faint, and sick, and dry,
And bloodshot was his fev'rish eye;
And livid was his lip, while he
Sate silent in the tall Elm tree—
And parch'd his tongue; and quick his breath,
And his dark cheek, was cold as Death!

XI.

And now a Cottage low he sees,
The chimney smoke, ascending grey,
Floats lightly on the morning breeze
And o'er the mountain glides away.
And now the Lark, on flutt'ring wings,
Its early Song, delighted sings;
And now, across the upland mead,
The Swains their flocks to shelter lead;
The shelt'ring woods, wave to and fro;
The yellow plains, far distant, glow;
And all things wake to life and joy,
All I but the famish'd Indian Boy!

XII.

And now the village throngs are seen,
Each lane is peopled, and the glen
From ev'ry op'ning path-way green,
Sends forth the busy hum of men.
They cross the meads, still, all alone,
They hear the wounded LASCAR groan!
Far off they mark the wretch, as he
Falls, senseless, from the tall Elm tree!
Swiftly they cross the river wide
And soon they reach the Elm tree's side,
But, ere the sufferer they behold,
His wither'd Heart, is DEAD, and COLD!

THE WIDOW's HOME

Close on the margin of a brawling brook
That bathes the low dell's bosom, stands a Cot;
O'ershadow'd by broad Alders. At its door
A rude seat, with an ozier canopy
Invites the weary traveller to rest.
'Tis a poor humble dwelling; yet within,
The sweets of joy domestic, oft have made
The long hour not unchearly, while the Moor
Was covered with deep snow, and the bleak blast
Swept with impetuous wing the mountain's brow!

On ev'ry tree of the near shelt'ring wood
The minstrelsy of Nature, shrill and wild,

Welcomes the stranger guest, and carolling
Love-songs, spontaneous, greets him merrily.
The distant hills, empurpled by the dawn
And thinly scatter'd with blue mists that float
On their bleak summits dimly visible,
Skirt the domain luxuriant, while the air
Breathes healthful fragrance. On the Cottage roof
The gadding Ivy, and the tawny Vine
Bind the brown thatch, the shelter'd winter-hut
Of the tame Sparrow, and the Red-breast bold.
There dwells the Soldier's Widow! young and fair
Yet not more fair than virtuous. Every day
She wastes the hour-glass, waiting his return,—
And every hour anticipates the day,
(Deceiv'd, yet cherish'd by the flatt'rer hope)
When she shall meet her Hero. On the Eve
Of Sabbath rest, she trims her little hut
With blossoms, fresh and gaudy, still, herself
The queen-flow'r of the garland! The sweet Rose
Of wood-wild beauty, blushing thro' her tears.
One little Son she has, a lusty Boy,
The darling of her guiltless, mourning heart,
The only dear and gay associate
Of her lone widowhood. His sun-burnt cheek
Is never blanch'd with fear, though he will climb
The broad oak's branches, and with brawny arm
Sever the limpid wave. In his blue eye
Beams all his mother's gentleness of soul;
While his brave father's warm intrepid heart
Throbs in his infant bosom. 'Tis a wight
Most valourous, yet pliant as the stem
Of the low vale-born lily, when the dew
Presses its perfum'd head. Eight years his voice
Has chear'd the homely hut, for he could lisp
Soft words of filial fondness, ere his feet
Could measure the smooth path-way.
On the hills
He watches the wide waste of wavy green
Tissued with orient lustre, till his eyes
Ache with the dazzling splendour, and the main,
Rolling and blazing, seems a second Sun!
And, if a distant whitening sail appears,
Skimming the bright horizon while the mast
Is canopied with clouds of dappled gold,
He homeward hastes rejoicing. An old Tree
Is his lone watch-tow'r; 'tis a blasted Oak
Which, from a vagrant Acorn, ages past,
Sprang up, to triumph like a Savage bold

Braving the Season's warfare. There he sits
Silent and musing the long Evening hour,
'Till the short reign of Sunny splendour fades
At the cold touch of twilight. Oft he sings;
Or from his oaten pipe, untiring pours
The tune mellifluous which his father sung,
When HE could only listen.
On the sands
That bind the level sea-shore, will he stray,
When morn unlocks the East, and flings afar
The rosy day-beam! There the boy will stop
To gather the dank weeds which ocean leaves
On the bleak strand, while winter o'er the main
Howls its nocturnal clamour. There again
He chaunts his Father's ditty. Never more
Poor mountain minstrel, shall thy bosom throb
To the sweet cadence! never more thy tear
Fall as the dulcet breathings give each word
Expression magical! Thy Father, Boy,
Sleeps on the bed of death! His tongue is mute,
His fingers have forgot their pliant art,
His oaten pipe will ne'er again be heard
Echoing along the valley! Never more
Will thy fond mother meet the balmy smile
Of peace domestic, or the circling arm
Of valour, temper'd by the milder joys
Of rural merriment. His very name
Is now forgotten! for no trophied tomb
Tells of his bold exploits; such heraldry
Befits not humble worth: For pomp and praise
Wait in the gilded palaces of Pride
To dress Ambition's Slaves. Yet, on his grave,
The unmark'd resting place of Valour's Sons,
The morning beam shines lust'rous; The meek flow'r
Still drops the twilight tear, and the night breeze
Moans melancholy music!
Then, to ME,
O! dearer far is the poor Soldier's grave,
The Widow's lone and unregarded Cot,
The brawling Brook, and the wide Alder-bough,
The ozier Canopy, and plumy choir,
Hymning the Morn's return, than the rich Dome
Of gilded Palaces! and sweeter far—
O! far more graceful! far more exquisite,
The Widow's tear bathing the living rose,
Than the rich ruby, blushing on the breast,
Of guilty greatness. Welcome then to me—
The WIDOW'S LOWLY HOME: The Soldier's HEIR;

The proud inheritor of Heav'n's best gifts—
The mind unshackled—and the guiltless Soul!

THE SHEPHERD'S DOG

I.

A Shepherd's Dog there was; and he
Was faithful to his master's will,
For well he lov'd his company,
Along the plain or up the hill;
All Seasons were, to him, the same
Beneath the Sun's meridian flame;
Or, when the wintry wind blew shrill and keen,
Still the Old Shepherd's Dog, was with his Master seen.

II.

His form was shaggy clothed; yet he
Was of a bold and faithful breed;
And kept his master company
In smiling days, and days of need;
When the long Ev'ning slowly clos'd,
When ev'ry living thing repos'd,
When e'en the breeze slept on the woodlands round,
The Shepherd's watchful Dog, was ever waking found.

III.

All night, upon the cold turf he
Contented lay, with list'ning care;
And though no stranger company,
Or lonely traveller rested there;
Old Trim was pleas'd to guard it still,
For 'twas his aged master's will;—
And so pass'd on the chearful night and day,
'Till the poor Shepherd's Dog, was very old, and grey.

IV.

Among the villagers was he
Belov'd by all the young and old,
For he was chearful company,

When the north-wind blew keen and cold;
And when the cottage scarce was warm,
While round it flew, the midnight storm,
When loudly, fiercely roll'd the swelling tide—
The Shepherd's faithful Dog, crept closely by his side.

V.

When Spring in gaudy dress would be,
Sporting across the meadows green,
He kept his master company,
And all amid the flow'rs was seen;
Now barking loud, now pacing fast,
Now, backward he a look would cast,
And now, subdu'd and weak, with wanton play,
Amid the waving grass, the Shepherd's Dog would stay.

VI.

Now, up the rugged path would he
The steep hill's summit slowly gain,
And still be chearful company,
Though shiv'ring in the pelting rain;
And when the brook was frozen o'er,
Or the deep snow conceal'd the moor,
When the pale moon-beams scarcely shed a ray,
The Shepherd's faithful Dog, would mark the dang'rous way.

VII.

On Sunday, at the old Yew Tree,
Which canopies the church-yard stile,
Forc'd from his master's company,
The faithful TRIM would mope awhile;
For then his master's only care
Was the loud Psalm, or fervent Pray'r,
And, 'till the throng the church-yard path retrod,
The Shepherd's patient guard, lay silent on the sod.

VIII

Near their small hovel stood a tree,
Where TRIM was ev'ry morning found—
Waiting his master's company,

And looking wistfully around;
And if, along the upland mead,
He heard him tune the merry reed,
O, then! o'er hedge and ditch, thro' brake and briar,
The Shepherd's dog would haste, with eyes that seem'd on fire.

IX.

And now he pac'd the valley, free,
And now he bounded o'er the dew,
For well his master's company
Would recompence his toil he knew;
And where a rippling rill was seen
Flashing the woody brakes between,
Fearless of danger, thro' the lucid tide,
The Shepherd's eager dog, yelping with joy, would glide.

X.

Full many a year, the same was he
His love still stronger every day,
For, in his master's company,
He had grown old, and very grey;
And now his sight grew dim: and slow
Up the rough mountain he would go,
And his loud bark, which all the village knew,
With ev'ry wasting hour, more faint, and peevish grew.

XI.

One morn, to the low mead went he,
Rous'd from his threshold-bed to meet
A gay and lordly company!
The Sun was bright, the air was sweet;
Old TRIM was watchful of his care,
His master's flocks were feeding there,
And, fearful of the hounds, he yelping stood
Beneath a willow Tree, that wav'd across the flood.

XII.

Old TRIM was urg'd to wrath; for he
Was guardian of the meadow bounds;
And, heedless of the company,

With angry snarl attack'd the hounds!
Some felt his teeth, though they were old,
For still his ire was fierce and bold,
And ne'er did valiant chieftain feel more strong
Than the Old Shepherd's dog, when daring foes among.

XIII.

The Sun was setting o'er the Sea
The breezes murmuring sad, and slow,
When a gay lordly company,
Came to the Shepherd's hovel low;
Their arm'd associates stood around
The sheep-cote fence's narrow bound,
While its poor master heard, with fix'd despair,
That TRIM, his friend, deem'd MAD, was doom'd to perish there!

XIV.

The kind old Shepherd wept, for he
Had no such guide, to mark his way,
And kneeling pray'd the company,
To let him live, his little day!
"For many a year my Dog has been
"The only friend these eyes have seen,
"We both are old and feeble, he and I—
"Together we have liv'd, together let us die!

XV.

"Behold his dim, yet speaking eye!
"Which ill befits his visage grim
"He cannot from your anger fly,
"For slow and feeble is old TRIM!
"He looks, as though he fain would speak,
"His beard is white—his voice is weak-
"He IS NOT MAD! O! then, in pity spare
"The only watchful friend, of my small fleecy care!"

XVI.

The Shepherd ceas'd to speak, for He
Leant on his maple staff, subdu'd;
While pity touch'd the company,

And all, poor TRIM with sorrow view'd:
Nine days upon a willow bed
Old TRIM was doom'd to lay his head,
Oppress'd and sever'd from his master's door,
Enough to make him MAD—were he not so before!

XVII.

But not forsaken yet, was he,
For ev'ry morn, at peep of day,
To keep his old friend company,
The lonely Shepherd bent his way:
A little boat, across the stream,
Which glitter'd in the sunny beam,
Bore him, where foes no longer could annoy,
Where TRIM stood yelping loud, and ALMOST MAD with joy!

XVIII.

Six days had pass'd and still was he
Upon the island left to roam,
When on the stream a wither'd tree
Was gliding rapid midst the foam!
The little Boat now onward prest,
Danc'd o'er the river's bounding breast,
Till dash'd impetuous, 'gainst the old tree's side,
The Shepherd plung'd and groan'd, then sunk amid the tide.

XIX.

Old TRIM, now doom'd his friend to see
Beating the foam with wasted breath,
Resolv'd to bear him company,
E'en in the icy arms of death;
Soon with exulting cries he bore
His feeble master to the shore,
And, standing o'er him, howl'd in cadence sad,
For, fear and fondness, now, had nearly made him MAD.

XX.

Together, still their flocks they tend,
More happy than the proudly great;
The Shepherd has no other friend—

No Lordly home, no bed of state!
But on a pallet, clean and low,
They hear, unmov'd, the wild winds blow,
And though they ne'er another spring may see;
The Shepherd, and his Dog, are chearful company.

THE FUGITIVE

Oft have I seen yon Solitary Man
Pacing the upland meadow. On his brow
Sits melancholy, mark'd with decent pride,
As it would fly the busy, taunting world,
And feed upon reflection. Sometimes, near
The foot of an old Tree, he takes his seat
And with the page of legendary lore
Cheats the dull hour, while Evening's sober eye
Looks tearful as it closes. In the dell
By the swift brook he loiters, sad and mute,
Save when a struggling sigh, half murmur'd, steals
From his wrung bosom. To the rising moon,
His eye rais'd wistfully, expression fraught,
He pours the cherish'd anguish of his Soul,
Silent yet eloquent: For not a sound
That might alarm the night's lone centinel,
The dull-eyed Owl, escapes his trembling lip,
Unapt in supplication. He is young,
And yet the stamp of thought so tempers youth,
That all its fires are faded. What is He?
And why, when morning sails upon the breeze,
Fanning the blue hill's summit, does he stay
Loit'ring and sullen, like a Truant boy,
Beside the woodland glen; or stretch'd along
On the green slope, watch his slow wasting form
Reflected, trembling, on the river's breast?
His garb is coarse and threadbare, and his cheek
Is prematurely faded. The check'd tear,
Dimming his dark eye's lustre, seems to say,
"This world is now, to me, a barren waste,
"A desart, full of weeds and wounding thorns,
"And I am weary: for my journey here
"Has been, though short, but chearless." Is it so?
Poor Traveller! Oh tell me, tell me all—
For I, like thee, am but a Fugitive
An alien from delight, in this dark scene!
And, now I mark thy features, I behold
The cause of thy complaining. Thou art here

A persecuted Exile! one, whose soul
Unbow'd by guilt, demands no patronage
From blunted feeling, or the frozen hand
Of gilded Ostentation. Thou, poor PRIEST!
Art here, a Stranger, from thy kindred torn-
Thy kindred massacred! thy quiet home,
The rural palace of some village scant,
Shelter'd by vineyards, skirted by fair meads,
And by the music of a shallow rill
Made ever chearful, now thou hast exchang'd
For stranger woods and vallies.

What of that!
Here, or on torrid desarts; o'er the world
Of trackless waves, or on the frozen cliffs
Of black Siberia, thou art not alone!
For there, on each, on all, The DEITY
Is thy companion still! Then, exiled MAN!
Be chearful as the Lark that o'er yon hill
In Nature's language, wild, yet musical,
Hails the Creator! nor thus, sullenly
Repine, that, through the day, the sunny beam
Of lust'rous fortune gilds the palace roof,
While thy short path, in this wild labyrinth,
Is lost in transient shadow.
Who, that lives,
Hath not his portion of calamity?
Who, that feels, can boast a tranquil bosom?
The fever, throbbing in the Tyrant's veins
In quick, strong language, tells the daring wretch
That He is mortal, like the poorest slave
Who wears his chain, yet healthfully suspires.

The sweetest Rose will wither, while the storm
Passes the mountain thistle. The bold Bird,
Whose strong eye braves the ever burning Orb,
Falls like the Summer Fly, and has at most,
But his allotted sojourn. EXILED MAN!
Be chearful! Thou art not a fugitive!
All are thy kindred-all thy brothers, here—
The hoping—trembling Creatures—of one GOD!

THE HAUNTED BEACH

Upon a lonely desert Beach
Where the white foam was scatter'd,

A little shed uprear'd its head
Though lofty Barks were shatter'd.
The Sea-weeds gath'ring near the door,
A sombre path display'd;
And, all around, the deaf'ning roar,
Re-echo'd on the chalky shore,
By the green billows made.

Above, a jutting cliff was seen
Where Sea Birds hover'd, craving;
And all around, the craggs were bound
With weeds—for ever waving.
And here and there, a cavern wide
Its shad'wy jaws display'd;
And near the sands, at ebb of tide,
A shiver'd mast was seen to ride
Where the green billows stray'd.

And often, while the moaning wind
Stole o'er the Summer Ocean;
The moonlight scene, was all serene,
The waters scarce in motion:
Then, while the smoothly slanting sand
The tall cliff wrapp'd in shade,
The Fisherman beheld a band
Of Spectres, gliding hand in hand—
Where the green billows play'd.

And pale their faces were, as snow,
And sullenly they wander'd:
And to the skies with hollow eyes
They look'd as though they ponder'd.
And sometimes, from their hammock shroud,
They dismal howlings made,
And while the blast blew strong and loud
The clear moon mark'd the ghastly croud,
Where the green billows play'd!

And then, above the haunted hut
The Curlews screaming hover'd;
And the low door with furious roar
The frothy breakers cover'd.
For, in the Fisherman's lone shed
A MURDER'D MAN was laid,
With ten wide gashes in his head
And deep was made his sandy bed
Where the green billows play'd.

A Shipwreck'd Mariner was he,
Doom'd from his home to sever;
Who swore to be thro' wind and sea
Firm and undaunted ever!
And when the wave resistless roll'd,
About his arm he made
A packet rich of Spanish gold,
And, like a British sailor, bold,
Plung'd, where the billows play'd!

The Spectre band, his messmates brave
Sunk in the yawning ocean,
While to the mast he lash'd him fast
And brav'd the storm's commotion.
The winter moon, upon the sand
A silv'ry carpet made,
And mark'd the Sailor reach the land,
And mark'd his murd'rer wash his hand
Where the green billows play'd.

And since that hour the Fisherman
Has toil'd and toil'd in vain!
For all the night, the moony light
Gleams on the specter'd main!
And when the skies are veil'd in gloom,
The Murd'rer's liquid way
Bounds o'er the deeply yawning tomb,
And flashing fires the sands illume,
Where the green billows play!

Full thirty years his task has been,
Day after day more weary;
For Heav'n design'd, his guilty mind
Should dwell on prospects dreary.
Bound by a strong and mystic chain,
He has not pow'r to stray;
But, destin'd mis'ry to sustain,
He wastes, in Solitude and Pain—
A loathsome life away.

OLD BARNARD, A MONKISH TALE

OLD BARNARD was still a lusty hind,
Though his age was full fourscore;
And he us'd to go
Thro' hail and snow,

To a neighb'ring town,
With his old coat brown,
To beg, at his GRANDSON'S door!

OLD BARNARD briskly jogg'd along,
When the hail and snow did fall;
And, whatever the day,
He was always gay,
Did the broad Sun glow,
Or the keen wind blow,
While he begg'd in his GRANDSON'S Hall.

His GRANDSON was a Squire, and he
Had houses, and lands, and gold;
And a coach beside,
And horses to ride,
And a downy bed
To repose his head,
And he felt not the winter's cold.

Old BARNARD had neither house nor lands,
Nor gold to buy warm array;
Nor a coach to carry,
His old bones weary
Nor beds of feather
In freezing weather,
To sleep the long nights away.

But BARNARD a quiet conscience had,
No guile did his bosom know;
And when Ev'ning clos'd,
His old bones repos'd,
Tho' the wintry blast
O'er his hovel past,
And he slept, while the winds did blow!

But his GRANDSON, he could never sleep
'Till the Sun began to rise;
For a fev'rish pain
Oppress'd his brain,
And he fear'd some evil
And dream'd of the Devil,
Whenever he clos'd his eyes!

And whenever he feasted the rich and gay,
The Devil still had his joke;
For however rare
The sumptuous fare,

When the sparkling glass
Was seen to pass,—
He was fearful the draught would choke!

And whenever, in fine and costly geer,
The Squire went forth to ride:
The owl would cry,
And the raven fly
Across his road,
While the sluggish toad
Would crawl by his Palfry's side.

And he could not command the Sunny day,
For the rain would wet him through;
And the wind would blow
Where his nag did go,
And the thunder roar,
And the torrents pour,
And he felt the chill Evening dew.

And the cramp would wring his youthful bones,
And would make him groan aloud;
And the doctor's art
Could not cure the heart,
While the conscience still
Was o'ercharg'd with ill;
And he dream'd of the pick-axe and shroud.

And why could Old BARNARD sweetly sleep,
Since so poor, and so old was he?
Because he could say
At the close of day,
"I have done no wrong
"To the weak or strong,
"And so, Heaven look kind on me!"

One night, the GRANDSON hied him forth,
To a MONK, that liv'd hard by;
"O! Father!" said he,
"I am come to thee,
"For I'm sick of sin,
"And would fain begin
"To repent me, before I die!"

"I must pray for your Soul; the MONK replied,
"But will see you to-morrow, ere noon:
Then the MONK flew straight
To Old BARNARD'S gate,

And he bade him haste
O'er the dewy waste,
By the light of the waning Moon.

In the Monkish cell did old BARNARD wait,
And his GRANDSON went thither soon;
In a habit of grey
Ere the dawn of day,
With a cowl and cross,
On the sill of moss,
He knelt by the light of the Moon.

"O! shrive me, Father!" the GRANDSON cried,
"For the Devil is waiting for me!
"I have robb'd the poor,
"I have shut my door,
"And kept out the good
"When they wanted food,—
"And I come for my pardon, to Thee."

"Get home young Sinner," Old BARNARD said,
And your GRANDSIRE quickly see;
"Give him half your store,
"For he's old, and poor,
"And avert each evil
"And cheat the Devil,—
By making him rich as thee."

The SQUIRE obey'd; and Old BARNARD now
Is rescued from every evil:
For he fears no wrong,
From the weak or strong,
And the Squire can snore,
When the loud winds roar,
For he dreams no more of THE DEVIL!

THE HERMIT OF MONT-BLANC

High, on the Solitude of Alpine Hills,
O'er-topping the grand imag'ry of Nature,
Where one eternal winter seem'd to reign;
An HERMIT'S threshold, carpetted with moss,
Diversified the Scene. Above the flakes
Of silv'ry snow, full many a modest flow'r
Peep'd through its icy veil, and blushing ope'd
Its variegated hues; The ORCHIS sweet,

The bloomy CISTUS, and the fragrant branch
Of glossy MYRTLE. In his rushy cell,
The lonely ANCHORET consum'd his days,
Unnotic'd, and unblest. In early youth,
Cross'd in the fond affections of his soul
By false Ambition, from his parent home
He, solitary, wander'd; while the Maid
Whose peerless beauty won his yielding heart
Pined in monastic horrors! Near his sill
A little cross he rear'd, where, prostrate low
At day's pale glimpse, or when the setting Sun
Tissued the western sky with streamy gold,
His Orisons he pour'd, for her, whose hours
Were wasted in oblivion. Winters pass'd,
And Summers faded, slow, unchearly all
To the lone HERMIT'S sorrows: For, still, Love
A dark, though unpolluted altar, rear'd
On the white waste of wonders!
From the peak
Which mark'd his neighb'ring Hut, his humid Eye
Oft wander'd o'er the rich expanse below;
Oft trac'd the glow of vegetating Spring,
The full-blown Summer splendours, and the hue
Of tawny scenes Autumnal: Vineyards vast,
Clothing the upland scene, and spreading wide
The promised tide nectareous; while for him
The liquid lapse of the slow brook was seen
Flashing amid the trees, its silv'ry wave!
Far distant, the blue mist of waters rose
Veiling the ridgy outline, faintly grey,
Blended with clouds, and shutting out the Sun.
The Seasons still revolv'd, and still was he
By all forgotten, save by her, whose breast
Sigh'd in responsive sadness to the gale
That swept her prison turrets. Five long years,
Had seen his graces wither ere his Spring
Of life was wasted. From the social scenes
Of human energy an alien driv'n,
He almost had forgot the face of Man.—
No voice had met his ear, save, when perchance
The Pilgrim wand'rer, or the Goatherd Swain,
Bewilder'd in the starless midnight hour
Implored the HERMIT'S aid, the HERMIT'S pray'rs;
And nothing loath by pity or by pray'r
Was he, to save the wretched. On the top
Of his low rushy Dome, a tinkling bell
Oft told the weary Trav'ller to approach
Fearless of danger. The small silver sound

In quick vibrations echo'd down the dell
To the dim valley's quiet, while the breeze
Slept on the glassy LEMAN. Thus he past
His melancholy days, an alien Man
From all the joys of social intercourse,
Alone, unpitied, by the world forgot!
His Scrip each morning bore the day's repast
Gather'd on summits, mingling with the clouds,
From whose bleak altitude the Eye look'd down
While fast the giddy brain was rock'd by fear.
Oft would he start from visionary rest
When roaming wolves their midnight chorus howl'd,
Or blasts infuriate shatter'd the white cliffs,
While the huge fragments, rifted by the storm,
Plung'd to the dell below. Oft would he sit
In silent sadness on the jutting block
Of snow-encrusted ice, and, shudd'ring mark
(Amid the wonders of the frozen world)
Dissolving pyramids, and threatening peaks,
Hang o'er his hovel, terribly Sublime.
And oft, when Summer breath'd ambrosial gales,
Soft sailing o'er the waste of printless dew
Or twilight gossamer, his pensive gaze
Trac'd the swift storm advancing, whose broad wing
Blacken'd the rushy dome of his low Hut;
While the pale lightning smote the pathless top
Of tow'ring CENIS, scatt'ring high and wide
A mist of fleecy Snow. Then would he hear,
(While MEM'RY brought to view his happier days)
The tumbling torrent, bursting wildly forth
From its thaw'd prison, sweep the shaggy cliff
Vast and Stupendous! strength'ning as it fell,
And delving, 'mid the snow, a cavern rude!

So liv'd the HERMIT, like an hardy Tree
Plac'd on a mountain's solitary brow,
And destin'd, thro' the Seasons, to endure
Their wond'rous changes. To behold the face
Of ever-varying Nature, and to mark
In each grand lineament, the work of GOD!
And happier he, in total Solitude
Than the poor toil-worn wretch, whose ardent Soul
That GOD has nobly organiz'd, but taught,
For purposes unknown, to bear the scourge
Of sharp adversity, and vulgar pride.
Happier, O! happier far, than those who feel,
Yet live amongst the unfeeling! feeding still
The throbbing heart, with anguish, or with Scorn.

One dreary night when Winter's icy breath
Half petrified the scene, when not a star
Gleam'd o'er the black infinity of space,
Sudden, the HERMIT started from his couch
Fear-struck and trembling! Ev'ry limb was shook
With painful agitation. On his cheek
The blanch'd interpreter of horror mute
Sat terribly impressive! In his breast
The ruddy fount of life convulsive flow'd
And his broad eyes, fix'd motionless as death,
Gaz'd vacantly aghast! His feeble lamp
Was wasting rapidly; the biting gale
Pierc'd the thin texture of his narrow cell;
And Silence, like a fearful centinel
Marking the peril which awaited near,
Conspir'd with sullen Night, to wrap the scene
In tenfold horrors. Thrice he rose; and thrice
His feet recoil'd; and still the livid flame
Lengthen'd and quiver'd as the moaning wind
Pass'd thro' the rushy crevice, while his heart
Beat, like the death-watch, in his shudd'ring breast.
Like the pale Image of Despair he sat,
The cold drops pacing down his hollow cheek,
When a deep groan assail'd his startled ear,
And rous'd him into action. To the sill
Of his low hovel he rush'd forth, (for fear
Will sometimes take the shape of fortitude,
And force men into bravery) and soon
The wicker bolt unfasten'd. The swift blast,
Now unrestrain'd, flew by; and in its course
The quiv'ring lamp extinguish'd, and again
His soul was thrill'd with terror. On he went,
E'en to the snow-fring'd margin of the cragg,
Which to his citadel a platform made
Slipp'ry and perilous! 'Twas darkness, all!
All, solitary gloom!—The concave vast
Of Heav'n frown'd chaos; for all varied things
Of air, and earth, and waters, blended, lost
Their forms, in blank oblivion! Yet not long
Did Nature wear her sable panoply,
For, while the HERMIT listen'd, from below
A stream of light ascended, spreading round
A partial view of trackless solitudes;
And mingling voices seem'd, with busy hum,
To break the spell of horrors. Down the steep
The HERMIT hasten'd, when a shriek of death
Re-echoed to the valley. As he flew,
(The treach'rous pathway yielding to his speed,)

Half hoping, half despairing, to the scene
Of wonder-waking anguish, suddenly
The torches were extinct; and second night
Came doubly hideous, while the hollow tongues
Of cavern'd winds, with melancholy sound
Increas'd the HERMIT'S fears. Four freezing hours
He watch'd and pray'd: and now the glimm'ring dawn
Peer'd on the Eastern Summits; (the blue light
Shedding cold lustre on the colder brows
Of Alpine desarts;) while the filmy wing
Of weeping Twilight, swept the naked plains
Of the Lombardian landscape.
On his knees
The ANCHORET blest Heav'n, that he had 'scap'd
The many perilous and fearful falls
Of waters wild and foamy, tumbling fast
From the shagg'd altitude. But, ere his pray'rs
Rose to their destin'd Heav'n, another sight,
Than all preceding far more terrible,
Palsied devotion's ardour. On the Snow,
Dappled with ruby drops, a track was made
By steps precipitate; a rugged path
Down the steep frozen chasm had mark'd the fate
Of some night traveller, whose bleeding form
Had toppled from the Summit. Lower still
The ANCHORET descended, 'till arrived
At the first ridge of silv'ry battlements,
Where, lifeless, ghastly, paler than the snow
On which her cheek repos'd, his darling Maid
Slept in the dream of Death! Frantic and wild
He clasp'd her stiff'ning form, and bath'd with tears
The lilies of her bosom,—icy cold—
Yet beautiful and spotless.
Now, afar
The wond'ring HERMIT heard the clang of arms
Re-echoing from the valley: the white cliffs
Trembled as though an Earthquake shook their base
With terrible concussion! Thund'ring peals
From warfare's brazen throat, proclaim'd th' approach
Of conquering legions: onward they extend
Their dauntless columns! In the foremost group
A Ruffian met the HERMIT'S startled Eyes
Like Hell's worst Demon! For his murd'rous hands
Were smear'd with gore; and on his daring breast
A golden cross, suspended, bore the name
Of his ill-fated Victim!—ANCHORET!
Thy VESTAL Saint, by his unhallow'd hands
Torn from RELIGION'S Altar, had been made

The sport of a dark Fiend, whose recreant Soul
Had sham'd the cause of Valour! To his cell
The Soul-struck Exile turn'd his trembling feet,
And after three lone weeks, of pain and pray'r,
Shrunk from the scene of Solitude—and DIED!

DEBORAH'S PARROT, A VILLAGE TALE

'Twas in a little western town
An ancient Maiden dwelt:
Her name was MISS, or MISTRESS, Brown,
Or DEBORAH, or DEBBY: She
Was doom'd a Spinster pure to be,
For soft delights her breast ne'er felt:
Yet, she had watchful Ears and Eyes
For ev'ry youthful neighbour,
And never did she cease to labour
A tripping female to surprize.

And why was she so wond'rous pure,
So stiff, so solemn-so demure?
Why did she watch with so much care
The roving youth, the wand'ring fair?
The tattler, Fame, has said that she
A Spinster's life had long detested,
But 'twas her quiet destiny,
Never to be molested!—
And had Miss DEBBY'S form been grac'd,
Fame adds,-She had not been so chaste;—
But since for frailty she would roam,
She ne'er was taught—to look at home.

Miss DEBBY was of mien demure
And blush'd, like any maid!
She could not saucy man endure
Lest she should be betray'd!
She never fail'd at dance or fair
To watch the wily lurcher's snare;
At Church, she was a model Godly!
Though sometimes she had other eyes
Than those, uplifted to the skies,
Leering most oddly!
And Scandal, ever busy, thought
She rarely practic'd—what she taught.

Her dress was always stiff brocade,

With laces broad and dear;
Fine Cobwebs! that would thinly shade
Her shrivell'd cheek of sallow hue,
While, like a Spider, her keen eye,
Which never shed soft pity's tear,
Small holes in others geer could spy,
And microscopic follies, prying view.
And sorely vex'd was ev'ry simple thing
That wander'd near her never-tiring sting!

Miss DEBBY had a PARROT, who,
If Fame speaks true,
Could prate, and tell what neighbours did,
And yet the saucy rogue was never chid!
Sometimes, he talk'd of roving Spouses
Who wander'd from their quiet houses:
Sometimes, he call'd a Spinster pure
By names, that Virtue can't indure!
And sometimes told an ancient Dame
Such tales as made her blush with shame!
Then gabbled how a giddy Miss
Would give the boist'rous Squire a kiss!
But chiefly he was taught to cry,
Who with the Parson toy'd? O fie!"

This little joke, Miss DEBBY taught him,
To vex a young and pretty neighbour;
But by her scandal-zealous labour
To shame she brought him!
For, the Old PARROT, like his teacher
Was but a false and canting preacher,
And many a gamesome pair had sworn
Such lessons were not to be borne.

At last, Miss DEBBY sore was flouted
And by her angry neighbours scouted;
She never knew one hour of rest,
Of ev'ry Saucy Boor, the jest:
The young despis'd her, and the Sage
Look'd back on Time's impartial page;
They knew that youth was giv'n to prove
The season of extatic joy,
That none but Cynics would destroy,
The early buds of love
They also knew that DEBBY sigh'd
For charms that envious Time deny'd;
That she was vex'd with jealous Spleen
That Hymen pass'd her by, unseen.

For though the Spinster's wealth was known,
Gold will not purchase Love-alone.
She, and her PARROT, now were thought
The torments of their little Sphere;
He, because mischievously taught,
And She, because a maid austere!—
In short, she deem'd it wise to leave
A Place, where none remain'd, to grieve.

Soon, to a distant town remov'd,
Miss DEBBY'S gold an husband bought;
And all she had her PARROT taught,
(Her PARROT now no more belov'd,)
Was quite forgotten. But, alas!
As Fate would have it come to pass,
Her Spouse was giv'n to jealous rage,
For, both in Person and in Age,
He was the partner of his love,
Ordain'd her second Self to prove!

One day, Old JENKINS had been out
With merry friends to dine,
And, freely talking, had, no doubt
Been also free with wine.
One said, of all the wanton gay
In the whole parish search it round,
None like the PARSON could be found,
Where a frail Maid was in the way.
Another thought the Parson sure
To win the heart of maid or wife;
And would have freely pledg'd his life
That young, or old, or rich or poor
None could defy
The magic of his roving eye!

JENKINS went home, but all the night
He dream'd of this strange tale!
Yet, bless'd his stars! with proud delight,
His partner was not young, nor frail.

Next morning, at the breakfast table.
The PARROT, loud as he was able,
Was heard repeatedly to cry,
Who with the Parson toy'd? O fie!"

Old JENKINS listen'd, and grew pale,
The PARROT then, more loudly scream'd,

And MISTRESS JENKINS heard the tale
And much alarm'd she seem'd!
Trembling she tried to stop his breath,
Her lips and cheek as pale as death!
The more she trembled, still the more
Old JENKINS view'd her o'er and o'er;
And now her yellow cheek was spread
With blushes of the deepest red.

And now again the PARROT'S Tale
Made his old Tutoress doubly pale;
For cowardice and guilt, they say
Are the twin brothers of the soul;

So MISTRESS JENKINS, her dismay
Could not controul!
While the accuser, now grown bold,
Thrice o'er, the tale of mischief told.

Now JENKINS from the table rose,
"Who with the Parson toy'd?" he cried.
"So MISTRESS FRAILTY, you must play,
"And sport, your wanton hours away.
"And with your gold, a pretty joke,
"You thought to buy a pleasant cloak;
"A screen to hide your shame-but know
"I will not blind to ruin go.—
"I am no modern Spouse, dy'e see,
"Gold will not gild disgrace, with me!"
Some say he seiz'd his fearful bride,
And came to blows!
Day after day, the contest dire
Augmented, with resistless ire!
And many a drubbing DEBBY bought
For mischief, she her PARROT taught!

Thus, SLANDER turns against its maker;
And if this little Story reaches
A SPINSTER, who her PARROT teaches,
Let her a better task pursue,
And here, the certain VENGEANCE view
Which surely will, in TIME, O'ERTAKE HER.

THE NEGRO GIRL

I.

Dark was the dawn, and o'er the deep
The boist'rous whirlwinds blew;
The Sea-bird wheel'd its circling sweep,
And all was drear to view—
When on the beach that binds the western shore
The love-lorn ZELMA stood, list'ning the tempest's roar.

II.

Her eager Eyes beheld the main,
While on her DRACO dear
She madly call'd, but call'd in vain,
No sound could DRACO hear,
Save the shrill yelling of the fateful blast,
While ev'ry Seaman's heart, quick shudder'd as it past.

III.

White were the billows, wide display'd
The clouds were black and low;
The Bittern shriek'd, a gliding shade
Seem'd o'er the waves to go!
The livid flash illum'd the clam'rous main,
While ZELMA pour'd, unmark'd, her melancholy strain.

IV.

"Be still!" she cried, "loud tempest cease!
"O! spare the gallant souls:
"The thunder rolls—the winds increase—
"The Sea, like mountains, rolls!
"While, from the deck, the storm worn victims leap,
"And o'er their struggling limbs, the furious billows sweep.

V.

"O! barb'rous Pow'r! relentless Fate!
"Does Heav'n's high will decree
"That some should sleep on beds of state,—
"Some, in the roaring Sea?
"Some, nurs'd in splendour, deal Oppression's blow,
"While worth and DRACO pine—in Slavery and woe!

VI.

"Yon Vessel oft has plough'd the main
"With human traffic fraught;
"Its cargo,-our dark Sons of pain—
"For worldly treasure bought!
"What had they done?—O Nature tell me why—
"Is taunting scorn the lot, of thy dark progeny?

VII.

"Thou gav'st, in thy caprice, the Soul
"Peculiarly enshrin'd;
"Nor from the ebon Casket stole
"The Jewel of the mind!
"Then wherefore let the suff'ring Negro's breast
"Bow to his fellow, MAN, in brighter colours drest.

VIII.

"Is it the dim and glossy hue
"That marks him for despair?—
"While men with blood their hands embrue,
"And mock the wretch's pray'r?
"Shall guiltless Slaves the Scourge of tyrants feel,
"And, e'en before their GOD! unheard, unpitied kneel.

IX.

"Could the proud rulers of the land
"Our Sable race behold;
"Some bow'd by torture's Giant hand
"And others, basely sold!
"Then would they pity Slaves, and cry, with shame,
"Whate'er their TINTS may be, their SOULS are still the same!

X.

"Why seek to mock tho Ethiop's face?
"Why goad our hapless kind?
"Can features alienate the race—
"Is there no kindred mind?
"Does not the cheek which vaunts the roseate hue

"Oft blush for crimes, that Ethiops never knew?

XI.

"Behold! the angry waves conspire
"To check the barb'rous toil!
"While wounded Nature's vengeful ire—
"Roars, round this trembling Isle!
"And hark! her voice re-echoes in the wind—
"Man was not form'd by Heav'n, to trample on his kind!

XII.

"Torn from my Mother's aching breast,
"My Tyrant sought my love—
"But, in the Grave shall ZELMA rest,
"E'er she will faithless prove—
"No DRACO!—Thy companion I will be
"To that celestial realm, where Negros shall be free!

XIII.

"The Tyrant WHITE MAN taught my mind-
"The letter'd page to trace;—
"He taught me in the Soul to find
"No tint, as in the face:
"He bade my Reason, blossom like the tree—
"But fond affection gave, the ripen'd fruits to thee.

XIV.

"With jealous rage he mark'd my love
"He sent thee far away;—
"And prison'd in the plantain grove—
"Poor ZELMA pass'd the day—
"But ere the moon rose high above the main,
"ZELMA, and Love contriv'd, to break the Tyrant's chain.

XV.

"Swift, o'er the plain of burning Sand
"My course I bent to thee;
"And soon I reach'd the billowy strand

"Which bounds the stormy Sea.—
"DRACO! my Love! Oh yet, thy ZELMA'S soul
"Springs ardently to thee,—impatient of controul.

XVI.

"Again the lightning flashes white—
"The rattling cords among!
"Now, by the transient vivid light,
"I mark the frantic throng!
"Now up the tatter'd shrouds my DRACO flies—
While o'er the plunging prow, the curling billows rise.

XVII.

"The topmast falls-three shackled slaves-
"Cling to the Vessel's side!
"Now lost amid the madd'ning waves—
"Now on the mast they ride—
"See! on the forecastle my DRACO stands
"And now he waves his chain, now clasps his bleeding hands.

XVIII.

"Why, cruel WHITE-MAN! when away
"My sable Love was torn,
"Why did you let poor ZELMA stay,
On Afric's sands to mourn?
"No! ZELMA is not left, for she will prove
"In the deep troubled main, her fond-her faithful LOVE."

XIX.

The lab'ring Ship was now a wreck,
The shrouds were flutt'ring wide!
The rudder gone, the lofty deck
Was rock'd from side to side—
Poor ZELMA'S eyes now dropp'd their last big tear,
While, from her tawny cheek, the blood recoil'd with fear.

XX.

Now frantic, on the sands she roam'd,

Now shrieking stop'd to view
Where high the liquid mountains foam'd,
Around the exhausted crew—
'Till, from the deck, her DRACO'S well known form
Sprung mid the yawning waves, and buffetted the Storm.

XXI.

Long, on the swelling surge sustain'd
Brave DRACO sought the shore,
Watch'd the dark Maid, but ne'er complain'd,
Then sunk, to gaze no more!
Poor ZELMA saw him buried by the wave—
And, with her heart's true Love, plung'd in a wat'ry grave.

THE TRUMPETER, AN OLD ENGLISH TALE

It was in the days of a gay British King
(In the old fashion'd custom of merry-making)
The Palace of Woodstock with revels did ring,
While they sang and carous'd-one and all:
For the monarch a plentiful treasury had,
And his Courtiers were pleas'd, and no visage was sad,
And the knavish and foolish with drinking were mad,
While they sat in the Banquetting hall.

Some talk'd of their Valour, and some of their Race,
And vaunted, till vaunting was black in the face;
Some bragg'd for a title, and some for a place,
And, like braggarts, they bragg'd one and all!
Some spoke of their scars in the Holy Crusade,
Some boasted the banner of Fame they display'd,
And some sang their Loves in the soft serenade
As they sat in the Banquetting hall.

And here sat a Baron, and there sat a Knight,
And here stood a Page in his habit all bright,
And here a young Soldier in armour bedight
With a Friar carous'd, one and all.
Some play'd on the dulcimer, some on the lute,
And some, who had nothing to talk of, were mute,
Till the Morning, awakened, put on her grey suit—
And the Lark hover'd over the Hall.

It was in a vast gothic Hall that they sate,

And the Tables were cover'd with rich gilded plate,
And the King and his minions were toping in state,
Till their noddles turn'd round, one and all:—
And the Sun through the tall painted windows 'gan peep,
And the Vassals were sleeping, or longing to sleep,
Though the Courtiers, still waking, their revels did keep,
While the minstrels play'd sweet, in the Hall.

And, now in their Cups, the bold topers began
To call for more wine, from the cellar yeoman,
And, while each one replenish'd his goblet or can,
The Monarch thus spake to them all:
"It is fit that the nobles do just what they please,
"That the Great live in idleness, riot, and ease,
"And that those should be favor'd, who mark my decrees,
"And should feast in the Banquetting Hall.

"It is fit," said the Monarch, "that riches should claim
"A passport to freedom, to honor, and fame,—
"That the poor should be humble, obedient, and tame,
"And, in silence, submit—one and all.
"That the wise and the holy should toil for the Great,
"That the Vassals should tend at the tables of state,
"That the Pilgrim should pray for our souls at the gate
"While we feast in our Banquetting Hall.

"That the low-lineag'd CARLES should be scantily fed—
"That their drink should be small, and still smaller their bread;
"That their wives and their daughters to ruin be led,
"And submit to our will, one and all!
"It is fit, that whoever I choose to defend—
"Shall be courted, and feasted, and lov'd as a friend,
"While before them the good and enlighten'd shall bend,
"While they sit in the Banquetting Hall."

Now the Topers grew bold, and each talk'd of his right,
One would fain be a Baron, another a Knight;
And another, (because at the Tournament fight
He had vanquished his foes, one and all)
Demanded a track of rich lands; and rich fare;
And of stout serving Vassals a plentiful share;
With a lasting exemption from penance and pray'r
And a throne in the Banquetting Hall.

But ONE, who had neither been valiant nor wise,
With a tone of importance, thus vauntingly cries,
"My Leige he knows how a good subject to prize—
"And I therefore demand-before all—

"I this Castle possess: and the right to maintain
"Five hundred stout Bowmen to follow my train,
"And as many strong Vassals to guard my domain
"As the Lord of the Banquetting Hall!

"I have fought with all nations, and bled in the field,
"See my lance is unshiver'd, tho' batter'd my shield,
"I have combatted legions, yet never would yield
"And the Enemy fled—one and all!
"I have rescued a thousand fair Donnas, in Spain,
"I have left in gay France, every bosom in pain.
"I have conquer'd the Russian, the Prussian, the Dane,
"And will reign in the Banquetting Hall!"

The Monarch now rose, with majestical look,
And his sword from the scabbard of Jewels he took,
And the Castle with laughter and ribaldry shook.
While the braggart accosted thus he:
"I will give thee a place that will suit thy demand,
"What to thee, is more fitting than Vassals or Land-
"I will give thee,—what justice and valour command,
"For a TRUMPETER bold—thou shalt be!"

Now the revellers rose, and began to complain-
While they menanc'd with gestures, and frown'd with disdain,
And declar'd, that the nobles were fitter to reign
Than a Prince so unruly as He.
But the Monarch cried, sternly, they taunted him so,
"From this moment the counsel of fools I forego-
"And on Wisdom and Virtue will honors bestow
"For such, ONLY, are welcome to Me!"

So saying, he quitted the Banquetting Hall,
And leaving his Courtiers and flatterers all—
Straightway for his Confessor loudly 'gan call
"O! Father! now listen!" said he:
"I have feasted the Fool, I have pamper'd the Knave,
"I have scoff'd at the wise, and neglected the brave—
"And here, Holy Man, Absolution I crave—
"For a penitent now I will be."

From that moment the Monarch grew sober and good,
(And nestled with Birds of a different brood,)
For he found that the pathway which wisdom pursu'd
Was pleasant, safe, quiet, and even!
That by Temperance, Virtue and liberal deeds,
By nursing the flowrets, and crushing the weeds,
The loftiest Traveller always succeeds—

For his journey will lead him to HEAV'N.

THE DESERTED COTTAGE

Who dwelt in yonder lonely Cot,
Why is it thus forsaken?
It seems, by all the world forgot,
Above its path the high grass grows,
And through its thatch the north-wind blows
Its thatch, by tempests shaken.

And yet, it tops a verdant hill
By Summer gales surrounded:
Beneath its door a shallow rill
Runs brawling to the vale below,
And near it sweetest flowrets grow
By banks of willow bounded.

Then why is ev'ry casement dark?
Why looks the Cot so chearless?
Ah! why does ruin seem to mark
The calm retreat where LOVE should dwell,
And FRIENDSHIP teach the heart to swell
With rapture, pure and fearless?

There, far above the busy croud,
Man may repose in quiet;
There, smile, that he has left the proud,
And blest with liberty, enjoy
More than Ambition's gilded toy,
Or Folly's sick'ning riot.

For there, the ever tranquil mind,
On calm Religion resting,
May in each lonely labyrinth find
The DEITY, whose boundless pow'r
Directs the blast, or tints the flow'r—
No mortal foe molesting.

Stranger, yon spot was once the scene
Where peace and joy resided:
And oft the merry time has been
When Love and Friendship warm'd the breast,
And Freedom, making wealth a jest,
The pride of Pomp derided.

Old JACOB was the Cottage Lord,
His wide domain, surrounding,
By Nature's treasure amply stor'd;
He from his casement could behold
The breezy mountain, ting'd with gold,
The varied landscape bounding!

The coming morn, with lustre gay,
Breath'd sweetly on his dwelling;
The twilight veil of parting day
Stole softly o'er his quiet shed,
Hiding the mountain's misty head,
Where the night-breeze was swelling.

One lovely Girl, Old JACOB rear'd
And she was fair, and blooming;
She, like the morning Star, appear'd,
Swift gliding o'er the mountain's crest,
While her blue eyes her soul confess'd,
No borrow'd rays assuming.

'Twas her's, the vagrant lamb to lead,
To watch the wild goat playing:
To join the Shepherd's tuneful reed,
And, when the sultry Sun rose high,
To tend the Herds, deep-lowing nigh,
Where the swift brook was straying.

One sturdy Boy, a younker bold,
Ere they were doom'd to sever,
Maintain'd poor JACOB, sick and old;
But now, where yon tall poplars wave,
Pale primroses adorn the grave—
Where JACOB sleeps, for Ever!

Young, in the wars, the brave Boy fell!
His Sister died of sadness!
But one remain'd their fate to tell,
For JACOB now was left alone,
And he, alas! was helpless grown,
And pin'd in moody madness.

At night, by moonshine would he stray,
Along the upland dreary;
And, talking wildly all the way,
Would fancy, 'till the Sun uprose,
That Heav'n, in pity, mark'd the woes—
Of which his soul was weary.

One morn, upon the dewy grass
Poor JACOB's sorrows ended,
The woodland's narrow winding pass
Was his last scene of lonely care,
For, gentle Stranger, lifeless there—
Was JACOB'S form extended!

He lies beneath yon Poplar tree
That tops the church-yard, sighing!
For sighing oft it seems to be,
And as its waving leaves, around,
With morning's tears begem the ground
The Zephyr trembles, flying!

And now behold yon little Cot
All dreary and forsaken!
And know, that soon 'twill be thy lot,
To fall, like Jacob and his race,
And leave on Time's swift wing no trace,
Which way thy course is taken.

Yet, if for Truth and feeling known,
Thou still shalt be lamented!
For when thy parting sigh has flown,
Fond MEM'RY on thy grave shall give
A tear—to bid thy VIRTUES live!
Then—Smile, AND BE CONTENTED!

THE FORTUNE-TELLER, A GYPSY TALE

LUBIN and KATE, as gossips tell,
Were Lovers many a day;
LUBIN the damsel lov'd so well,
That folks pretend to say
The silly, simple, doting Lad,
Was little less than loving mad:
A malady not known of late—
Among the little-loving Great!
KATE liked the youth; but woman-kind
Are sometimes giv'n to range.
And oft, the giddy Sex, we find,
(They know not why)
When most they promise, soonest change,
And still for conquest sigh:
So 'twas with KATE; she, ever roving

Was never fix'd, though always loving!
STEPHEN was LUBIN'S rival; he
A rustic libertine was known;
And many a blushing simple She,
The rogue had left,—to sigh alone!
KATE cared but little for the rover,
Yet she resolv'd to have her way,
For STEPHEN was the village Lover,
And women pant for Sov'reign sway.
And he, who has been known to ruin,—
Is always sought, and always wooing.

STEPHEN had long in secret sigh'd;
And STEPHEN never was deny'd:
Now, LUBIN was a modest swain,
And therefore, treated with disdain:
For, it is said, in Love and War,—
The boldest, most successful are!

Vows, were to him but fairy things
Borne on capricious Fancy's wings;
And promises, the Phantom's Airy
Which falsehood form'd to cheat th' unwary;
For still deception was his trade,
And though his traffic well was known,
Still, every trophy was his own
Which the proud Victor, Love, display'd.
In short, this STEPHEN was the bane
Of ev'ry maid,—and ev'ry swain!

KATE had too often play'd the fool,
And now, at length, was caught;
For she, who had been pleas'd to rule,
Was now, poor Maiden, taught!
And STEPHEN rul'd with boundless sway,
The rustic tyrant of his day.

LUBIN had giv'n inconstant KATE,
Ten pounds, to buy her wedding geer:
And now, 'tis said, tho' somewhat late,
He thought his bargain rather dear.
For, Lo! The day before the pair
Had fix'd, the marriage chain to wear,
A GYPSY gang, a wand'ring set,
In a lone wood young LUBIN met.
All round him press with canting tale,
And, in a jargon, well design'd
To cheat the unsuspecting mind,

His list'ning ears assail.

Some promis'd riches; others swore
He should, by women, be ador'd;
And never sad, and never poor—
Live like a Squire, or Lord;—
Do what he pleas'd, and ne'er be brought
To shame,—for what he did, or thought;
Seduce mens wives and daughters fair,
Spend wealth, while others toil'd in vain,
And scoff at honesty, and swear,—
And scoff, and trick, and swear again!

ONE roguish Girl, with sparkling eyes,
To win the handsome LUBIN tries;
She smil'd, and by her speaking glance,
Enthrall'd him in a wond'ring trance;
He thought her lovelier far than KATE,
And wish'd that she had been his mate;
For when the FANCY is on wing,
VARIETY'S a dangerous thing:
And PASSIONS, when they learn to stray
Will seldom seldom keep the beaten way.

The gypsy-girl, with speaking eyes,
Observ'd her pupil's fond surprize,
She begg'd that he her hand would cross,
With Sixpence; and that He should know
His future scene of gain and loss,
His weal and woe.—

LUBIN complies. And straight he hears
That he had many long, long years;
That he a maid inconstant, loves,
Who, to another slyly roves.
That a dark man his bane will be—
"And poison his domestic hours;
"While a fair woman, treach'rously—
"Will dress his brow—with thorns and flow'rs!"
It happen'd, to confirm his care—
STEPHEN was dark,—and KATE was fair!
Nay more that "home his bride would bring
"A little, alien, prattling thing
"In just six moons!" Poor LUBIN hears
All that confirms his jealous fears;
Perplex'd and frantic, what to do
The cheated Lover scarcely knew.
He flies to KATE, and straight he tells

The wonder that in magic dwells!
Speaks of the Fortune-telling crew,
And how all things the Vagrants knew;
KATE hears: and soon determines, she
Will know her future destiny.

Swift to the wood she hies, tho' late
To read the tablet of her Fate.
The Moon its crystal beam scarce shew'd
Upon the darkly shadow'd road;
The hedge-row was the feasting-place
Where, round a little blazing wood,
The wand'ring, dingy, gabbling race,
Crowded in merry mood.

And now she loiter'd near the scene.
Now peep'd the hazle copse between;
Fearful that LUBIN might be near
The story of her Fate to hear.—
She saw the feasting circle gay
By the stol'n faggot's yellow light;
She heard them, as in sportive play,
They chear'd the sullen gloom of night.
Nor was sly KATE by all unseen
Peeping, the hazle copse between.

And now across the thicket side
A tatter'd, skulking youth she spied;
He beckon'd her along, and soon,
Hid safely from the prying moon,
His hand with silver, thrice she crosses—
"Tell me," said she, "my gains and losses?"

"You gain a fool," the youth replies,
"You lose a lover too."
The false one blushes deep, and sighs,
For well the truth she knew!
"You gave to STEPHEN, vows; nay more
"You gave him favors rare:
"And LUBIN is condemn'd to share
"What many others shar'd before!
"A false, capricious, guilty heart,
"Made up of folly, vice, and art,
"Which only takes a wedded mate
"To brand with shame, an husband's fate."

"Hush! hush!" cried KATE, for Heav'n's sake be
"As secret as the grave-

"For LUBIN means to marry me—
"And if you will not me betray,
"I for your silence well will pay;
"Five pounds this moment you shall have."—
"I will have TEN!" the gypsy cries-
"The fearful, trembling girl complies.

But, what was her dismay, to find
That LUBIN was the gypsy bold;
The cunning, fortune-telling hind
Who had the artful story told—
Who thus, was cur'd of jealous pain,—
"And got his TEN POUNDS back again!

Thus, Fortune pays the LOVER bold!
But, gentle Maids, should Fate
Have any secret yet untold,—
Remember, simple KATE!

POOR MARGUERITE

Swift, o'er the wild and dreary waste
A NUT-BROWN GIRL was seen to haste;
Wide waving was her unbound hair,
And sun-scorch'd was her bosom bare;
For Summer's noon had shed its beams
While she lay wrapp'd in fev'rish dreams;
While, on the wither'd hedge-row's side,
By turns she slept, by turns she cried,
"Ah! where lies hid the balsam sweet,
"To heal the wounds of MARGUERITE?"

Dark was her large and sunken eye
Which wildly gaz'd upon the sky;
And swiftly down her freckled face
The chilling dews began to pace:
For she was lorn, and many a day,
Had, all alone, been doom'd to stray,
And, many a night, her bosom warm,
Had throbb'd, beneath the pelting storm,
And still she cried, "the rain falls sweet,
"It hathes the wounds of MARGUERITE."

Her garments were by briars torn,
And on them hung full many a thorn;
A thistle crown, she mutt'ring twin'd,

Now darted on,—now look'd behind—
And here, and there, her arm was seen
Bleeding the tatter'd folds between;
Yet, on her breast she oft display'd
A faded branch, that breast to shade:
For though her senses were astray,
She felt the burning beams of day:
She felt the wintry blast of night,
And smil'd to see the morning light,
For then she cried, "I soon shall meet
"The plighted love of MARGUERITE."

Across the waste of printless snow,
All day the NUT-BROWN GIRL would go;
And when the winter moon had shed
Its pale beams on the mountain's head,
She on a broomy pillow lay
Singing the lonely hours away;
While the cold breath of dawnlight flew
Across the fields of glitt'ring dew:—
Swift o'er the frozen lake she past
Unmindful of the driving blast,
And then she cried "the air is sweet—
"It fans the breast of MARGUERITE."

The weedy lane she lov'd to tread
When stars their twinkling lustre shed;
While from the lone and silent Cot
The watchful Cur assail'd her not,
Though at the beggar he would fly,
And fright the Trav'ller passing by:
But she, so kind and gentle seem'd,
Such sorrow in her dark eyes beam'd,
That savage fierceness could not greet
With less than love,-POOR MARGUERITE!

Oft, by the splashy brook she stood
And sung her Song to the waving wood;
The waving wood, in murmurs low,
Fill'd up the pause of weary woe;
Oft, to the Forest tripp'd along
And inly humm'd her frantic Song;
Oft danc'd mid shadows Ev'ning spread
Along the whisp'ring willow-bed.
And wild was her groan,
When she climb'd, alone—
The rough rock's side,
While the foaming tide,

Dash'd rudely against the sandy shore,
And the lightning flash'd mid the thunder's roar.

And many a time she chac'd the fly,
And mock'd the Beetle, humming by;
And then, with loud fantastic tone
She sang her wild strain, sad—alone.
And if a stranger wander'd near
Or paus'd the frantic Song to hear,
The burthen she would soft repeat,
"Who comes to soothe POOR MARGUERITE?

And why did she with sun-burnt breast,
So wander, and so scorn to rest?
Why did the NUT-BROWN MAIDEN go
O'er burning plains and wastes of snow?
What bade her fev'rish bosom sigh,
And dimm'd her large and hazle eye?
What taught her o'er the hills to stray
Fearless by night, and wild by day?

What stole the hour of slumber sweet—
From the scorch'd brain of MARGUERITE.

Soon shalt thou know; for see how lorn
She climbs the steep of shaggy thorn—
Now on the jutting cliff she stands,
And clasps her cold,—but snow-white hands.
And now aloud she chaunts her strain
While fiercely roars the troublous main.
Now the white breakers curling shew
The dread abyss that yawns below,
And still she sighs, "the sound is sweet,
"It seems to say, POOR MARGUERITE!"

"Here will I build a rocky shed,
"And here I'll make my sea-weed bed;
"Here gather, with unwearied hands—
"The orient shells that deck the sands.
"And here will I skim o'er the billows so high,
"And laugh at the moon and the dark frowning sky.

"And the Sea-birds, that hover across the wide main,
"Shall sweep with their pinions, the white bounding plain.—
"And the shivering sail shall the fierce tempest meet,
"Like the storm, in the bosom of POOR MARGUERITE!

"The setting Sun, with golden ray,

"Shall warm my breast, and make me gay.
"The clamours of the roaring Sea
"My midnight serenade shall be!
"The Cliff that like a Tyrant stands
"Exulting o'er the wave lash'd sands,
"With its weedy crown, and its flinty crest,
"Shall, on its hard bosom, rock me to rest;
"And I'll watch for the Eagle's unfledg'd brood,
"And I'll scatter their nest, and I'll drink their blood;
"And under the crag I will kneel and pray
"And silver my robe, with the moony ray:
"And who shall scorn the lone retreat
"Which Heaven has chose, for MARGUERITE?

"Here, did the exil'd HENRY stray
"Forc'd from his native land, away;
"Here, here upon a foreign shore,
"His parents, lost, awhile deplore;
"Here find, that pity's holy tear
"Could not an alien wand'rer chear;
"And now, in fancy, he would view,
"Shouting aloud, the rabble crew-
"The rabble crew, whose impious hands
"Tore asunder nature's bands!—
"I see him still,—He waves me on!
"And now to the dark abyss he's gone—
"He calls—I hear his voice, so sweet,—
"It seems to say—POOR MARGUERITE!"

Thus, wild she sung! when on the sand
She saw her long lost HENRY, stand:
Pale was his cheek, and on his breast
His icy hand he, silent, prest;
And now the Twilight shadows spread
Around the tall cliff's weedy head;
Far o'er the main the moon shone bright,
She mark'd the quiv'ring stream of light—
It danc'd upon the murm'ring wave
It danc'd upon—her HENRY'S Grave!
It mark'd his visage, deathly pale,—
His white shroud floating in the gale;
His speaking eyes—his smile so sweet
That won the love—of MARGUERITE!

And now he beckon'd her along
The curling moonlight waves among;
No footsteps mark'd the slanting sand
Where she had seen her HENRY stand!

She saw him o'er the billows go—
She heard the rising breezes blow;
She shriek'd aloud! The echoing steep
Frown'd darkness on the troubled deep;

The moon in cloudy veil was seen,
And louder howl'd the night blast keen!—
And when the morn, in splendour dress'd,
Blush'd radiance on the Eagle's nest,
That radiant blush was doom'd to greet—
The lifeless form—of MARGUERITE!

THE CONFESSOR, A SANCTIFIED TALE

When SUPERSTITION rul'd the land
And Priestcraft shackled Reason,
At GODSTOW dwelt a goodly band,
Grey monks they were, and but to say
They were not always giv'n to pray,
Would have been construed Treason.
Yet some did scoff, and some believ'd
That sinners were themselves deceiv'd;
And taking Monks for more than men
They prov'd themselves, nine out of ten,
Mere dupes of these Old Fathers hoary;
But read—and mark the story.

Near, in a little Farm, there liv'd
A buxom Dame of twenty three;
And by the neighbours 'twas believ'd
A very Saint was She!
Yet, ev'ry week, for some transgression,
She went to sigh devout confession.
For ev'ry trifle seem'd to make
Her self-reproving Conscience ache;
And Conscience, waken'd, 'tis well known,
Will never let the Soul alone.

At GODSTOW, 'mid the holy band,
Old FATHER PETER held command.
And lusty was the pious man,
As any of his crafty clan:
And rosy was his cheek, and sly
The wand'rings of his keen grey eye;
Yet all the Farmers wives confest
The wond'rous pow'r this Monk possess'd;

Pow'r to rub out the score of sin,
Which SATAN chalk'd upon his Tally;
To give fresh licence to begin,—
And for new scenes of frolic, rally.
For abstinence was not his way—
He lov'd to live-as well as pray;
To prove his gratitude to Heav'n
By taking freely all its favors,—
And keeping his account still even,
Still mark'd his best endeavours:
That is to say, He took pure Ore
For benedictions,—and was known,
While Reason op'd her golden store,—
Not to unlock his own.—
And often to his cell went he
With the gay Dame of twenty-three:
His Cell was sacred, and the fair
Well knew, that none could enter there,
Who, (such was PETER'S sage decree,)
To Paradise ne'er bought a key.

It happen'd that this Farmer's wife
(Call MISTRESS TWYFORD—alias BRIDGET,)
Led her poor spouse a weary life-
Keeping him, in an endless fidget!
Yet ev'ry week she sought the cell
Where Holy FATHER PETER stay'd,
And there did ev'ry secret tell,—
And there, at Sun-rise, knelt and pray'd.
For near, there liv'd a civil friend,
Than FARMER TWYFORD somewhat stouter,
And he would oft his counsel lend,
And pass the wintry hours away
In harmless play;
But MISTRESS BRIDGET was so chaste,
So much with pious manners grac'd,
That none could doubt her!

One night, or rather morn, 'tis said
The wily neighbour chose to roam,
And (FARMER TWYFORD far from home),
He thought he might supply his place;
And, void of ev'ry spark of grace,
Upon HIS pillow, rest his head.
The night was cold, and FATHER PETER,
Sent his young neighbour to entreat her,
That she would make confession free—
To Him,—his saintly deputy.

Now, so it happen'd, to annoy
The merry pair, a little boy
The only Son of lovely Bridget,
And, like his daddy, giv'n to fidget,
Enquir'd who this same neighbour was
That took the place his father left—
A most unworthy, shameless theft,—
A sacrilege on marriage laws!

The dame was somewhat disconcerted-
For, all that she could say or do,—
The boy his question would renew,
Nor from his purpose be diverted.

At length, the matter to decide,
"'Tis FATHER PETER" she replied.
"He's come to pray." The child gave o'er,
When a loud thumping at the door
Proclaim'd the Husband coming! Lo!
Where could the wily neighbour go?
Where hide his recreant, guilty head—
But underneath the Farmer's bed?—

NOW MASTER TWYFORD kiss'd his child;
And straight the cunning urchin smil'd:
"Hush father! hush! 'tis break of day—
"And FATHER PETER'S come to pray!
"You must not speak," the infant cries—
"For underneath the bed he lies."

Now MISTRESS TWYFORD shriek'd, and fainted,
And the sly neighbour found, too late,
The FARMER, than his wife less sainted,
For with his cudgel he repaid—
The kindness of his faithless mate,
And fiercely on his blows he laid,
'Till her young lover, vanquish'd, swore
He'd play THE CONFESSOR no more!

Tho' fraud is ever sure to find
Its scorpion in the guilty mind:
Yet, PIOUS FRAUD, the DEVIL'S treasure,
Is always paid, in TENFOLD MEASURE.

By the side of the brook, where the willow is waving
Why sits the wan Youth, in his wedding-suit gay!
Now sighing so deeply, now frantickly raving
Beneath the pale light of the moon's sickly ray.
Now he starts, all aghast, and with horror's wild gesture,
Cries, "AGNES is coming, I know her white vesture!
"See! see! how she beckons me on to the willow,
"Where, on the cold turf, she has made our rude pillow.

"Sweet girl! yes I know thee; thy cheek's living roses
"Are chang'd and grown pale, with the touch of despair:
"And thy bosom no longer the lily discloses-
"For thorns, my poor AGNES, are now planted there!
"Thy blue, starry Eyes! are all dimm'd by dark sorrow;
"No more from thy lip, can the flow'r fragrance borrow;
"For cold does it seem, like the pale light of morning,
"And thou smil'st, as in sadness, thy fond lover, scorning!

"From the red scene of slaughter thy Edmund returning,
"Has dress'd himself gayly, with May-blooming flow'rs;
"His bosom, dear AGNES! still faithfully burning,
"While, madly impatient, his eyes beam in show'rs!
"O! many a time have I thought of thy beauty—
"When cannons, loud roaring, taught Valour its duty;
"And many a time, have I sigh'd to behold thee—
"When the sulphur of War, in its cloudy mist roll'd me!

"At the still hour of morn, when the Camp was reposing,
"I wander'd alone on the wide dewy plain:
"And when the gold curtains of Ev'ning were closing,
"I watch'd the long shadows steal over the Main!
"Across the wild Ocean, half frantic they bore me,
"Unheeding my groans, from Thee, AGNES, they tore me;
"But, though my poor heart might have bled in the battle,
"Thy name should have echoed, amidst the loud rattle!

"When I gaz'd on the field of the dead and the dying-
"O AGNES! my fancy still wander'd to Thee!
"When around, my brave Comrades in anguish were lying,
"I long'd on the death-bed of Valour to be.
"For, sever'd from THEE, my SWEET GIRL, the loud thunder
"Which tore the soft fetters of fondness asunder—
"Had only one kindness, in mercy to shew me,
"To bid me die bravely, that thou, Love, may'st know me!

His arms now are folded, he bows as in sorrow,
His tears trickle fast, down his wedding-suit gay;
"My AGNES will bless me," he murmurs, "to-morrow,

"As fresh as the breezes that welcome the day!"
Poor Youth! know thy AGNES, so lovely and blooming,
Stern Death has embrac'd, all her beauties entombing!
And, pale as her shroud in the grave she reposes,
Her bosom of snow, all besprinkled with Roses!

Her Cottage is now in the dark dell decaying,
And shatter'd the casements, and clos'd is the door,
And the nettle now waves, where the wild KID is playing,
And the neat little garden with weeds is grown o'er!
The Owl builds its nest in the thatch, and there, shrieking,
(A place all deserted and lonely bespeaking)
Salutes the night traveller, wandering near it,
And makes his faint heart, sicken sadly to hear it.

Then Youth, for thy habit, henceforth, thou should'st borrow
The Raven's dark colour, and mourn for thy dear:
Thy AGNES for thee, would have cherish'd her Sorrow,
And drest her pale cheek with a lingering tear:
For, soon as thy steps to the Battle departed,
She droop'd, and poor Maiden! she died, broken hearted
And the turf that is bound with fresh garlands of roses,
Is now the cold bed, where her sorrow reposes!

The gay and the giddy may revel in pleasure,—
May think themselves happy, their short summer-day;
May gaze, with fond transport, on fortune's rich treasure,
And, carelessly sporting,—drive sorrow away:
But the bosom, where feeling and truth are united—
From folly's bright tinsel will turn, undelighted—
And find, at the grave where thy AGNES is sleeping,
That the proudest of hours, is the lone hour of weeping!

The Youth now approach'd the long branch of the willow,
And stripping its leaves, on the turf threw them round.
"Here, here, my sweet AGNES! I make my last pillow,
"My bed of long slumber, shall be the cold ground!
"The Sun, when it rises above thy low dwelling,
"Shall gild the tall Spire, where my death-toll is knelling.
"And when the next twilight its soft tears is shedding,
"At thy Grave shall the Villagers—witness our WEDDING!

Now over the Hills he beheld a group coming,
Their arms glitter'd bright, as the Sun slowly rose,
He heard them their purposes, far distant, humming,
And welcom'd the moment, that ended his woes!—
And now the fierce Comrade, unfeeling, espies him,
He darts thro' the thicket, in hopes to surprize him;

But EDMUND, of Valour the dauntless defender,
Now smiles, while his CORPORAL bids him—"SURRENDER!"

Soon, prov'd a DESERTER, Stern Justice prevailing,
HE DIED! and his Spirit to AGNES is fled:—
The breeze, on the mountain's tall summit now sailing
Fans lightly the dew-drops, that spangle their bed!
The Villagers, thronging around, scatter roses,
The grey wing of Evening the western sky closes,—
And Night's sable pall, o'er the landscape extending,
Is the mourning of Nature! the SOLEMN SCENE ENDING.

THE ALIEN BOY

'Twas on a Mountain, near the Western Main
An ALIEN dwelt. A solitary Hut
Built on a jutting crag, o'erhung with weeds,
Mark'd the poor Exile's home. Full ten long years
The melancholy wretch had liv'd unseen
By all, save HENRY, a lov'd, little Son
The partner of his sorrows. On the day
When Persecution, in the sainted guise
Of Liberty, spread wide its venom'd pow'r,
The brave, Saint HUBERT, fled his Lordly home,
And, with his baby Son, the mountain sought.

Resolv'd to cherish in his bleeding breast
The secret of his birth, Ah! birth too high
For his now humbled state, from infancy
He taught him, labour's task: He bade him chear
The dreary day of cold adversity
By patience and by toil. The Summer morn
Shone on the pillow of his rushy bed;
The noontide, sultry hour, he fearless past
On the shagg'd eminence; while the young Kid
Skipp'd, to the cadence of his minstrelsy.
At night young HENRY trimm'd the faggot fire
While oft, Saint HUBERT, wove the ample net
To snare the finny victim. Oft they sang
And talk'd, while sullenly the waves would sound
Dashing the sandy shore. Saint HUBERT'S eyes
Would swim in tears of fondness, mix'd with joy,
When he observ'd the op'ning harvest rich
Of promis'd intellect, which HENRY'S soul,

Whate'er the subject of their talk, display'd.

Oft, the bold Youth, in question intricate,
Would seek to know the story of his birth;
Oft ask, who bore him: and with curious skill
Enquire, why he, and only one beside,
Peopled the desert mountain? Still his Sire
Was slow of answer, and, in words obscure,
Varied the conversation. Still the mind
Of HENRY ponder'd; for, in their lone hut,
A daily journal would Saint HUBERT make
Of his long banishment: and sometimes speak
Of Friends forsaken, Kindred, massacred;—
Proud mansions, rich domains, and joyous scenes
For ever faded,—lost!
One winter time,
'Twas on the Eve of Christmas, the shrill blast
Swept o'er the stormy main. The boiling foam
Rose to an altitude so fierce and strong
That their low hovel totter'd. Oft they stole
To the rock's margin, and with fearful eyes
Mark'd the vex'd deep, as the slow rising moon
Gleam'd on the world of waters. 'Twas a scene
Would make a Stoic shudder! For, amid
The wavy mountains, they beheld, alone,
A LITTLE BOAT, now scarcely visible;
And now not seen at all; or, like a buoy,
Bounding, and buffetting, to reach the shore!
Now the full Moon, in crimson lustre shone
Upon the outstretch'd Ocean. The black clouds
Flew stiffly on, the wild blast following,
And, as they flew, dimming the angry main
With shadows horrible! Still, the small boat
Struggled amid the waves, a sombre speck
Upon the wide domain of howling Death!
Saint HUBERT sigh'd! while HENRY'S speaking eye
Alternately the stormy scene survey'd
And his low hovel's safety. So past on
The hour of midnight,—and, since first they knew
The solitary scene, no midnight hour
E'er seem'd so long and weary.
While they stood,
Their hands fast link'd together, and their eyes
Fix'd on the troublous Ocean, suddenly
The breakers, bounding on the rocky shore,
Left the small wreck; and crawling on the side
Of the rude crag,-a HUMAN FORM was seen!
And now he climb'd the foam-wash'd precipice,
And now the slip'ry weeds gave way, while he
Descended to the sands: The moon rose high—

The wild blast paus'd, and the poor shipwreck'd Man
Look'd round aghast, when on the frowning steep
He marked the lonely exiles. Now he call'd
But he was feeble, and his voice was lost
Amid the din of mingling sounds that rose
From the wild scene of clamour.
Down the steep
Saint HUBERT hurried, boldly venturous,
Catching the slimy weeds, from point to point,
And unappall'd by peril. At the foot
Of the rude rock, the fainting mariner
Seiz'd on his outstretch'd arm; impatient, wild,
With transport exquisite! But ere they heard
The blest exchange of sounds articulate,
A furious billow, rolling on the steep,
Engulph'd them in Oblivion!
On the rock
Young HENRY stood; with palpitating heart,
And fear-struck, e'en to madness! Now he call'd,
Louder and louder, as the shrill blast blew;
But, mid the elemental strife of sounds,
No human voice gave answer! The clear moon
No longer quiver'd on the curling main,
But, mist-encircled, shed a blunted light,
Enough to shew all things that mov'd around,
Dreadful, but indistinctly! The black weeds
Wav'd, as the night-blast swept them; and along
The rocky shore the breakers, sounding low
Seem'd like the whisp'ring of a million souls
Beneath the green-deep mourning.
Four long hours
The lorn Boy listen'd! four long tedious hours
Pass'd wearily away, when, in the East
The grey beam coldly glimmer'd. All alone
Young HENRY stood aghast: his Eye wide fix'd;
While his dark locks, uplifted by the storm
Uncover'd met its fury. On his cheek
Despair sate terrible! For, mid the woes,
Of poverty and toil, he had not known,
Till then, the horror-giving chearless hour
Of TOTAL SOLITUDE!

He spoke—he groan'd,
But no responsive voice, no kindred tone
Broke the dread pause: For now the storm had ceas'd,
And the bright Sun-beams glitter'd on the breast
Of the green placid Ocean. To his Hut
The lorn Boy hasten'd; there the rushy couch,

The pillow still indented, met his gaze
And fix'd his eye in madness.—From that hour
A maniac wild, the Alien Boy has been;
His garb with sea-weeds fring'd, and his wan cheek
The tablet of his mind, disorder'd, chang'd,
Fading, and worn with care. And if, by chance,
A Sea-beat wand'rer from the outstretch'd main
Views the lone Exile, and with gen'rous zeal
Hastes to the sandy beach, he suddenly
Darts 'mid the cavern'd cliffs, and leaves pursuit
To track him, where no footsteps but his own,
Have e'er been known to venture! YET HE LIVES
A melancholy proof that Man may bear
All the rude storms of Fate, and still suspire
By the wide world forgotten!

THE GRANNY GREY, A LOVE TALE

Dame Dowson, was a granny grey,
Who, three score years and ten,
Had pass'd her busy hours away,
In talking of the Men!
They were her theme, at home, abroad,
At wake, and by the winter fire,
Whether it froze, or blew, or thaw'd,
In sunshine or in shade, her ire
Was never calm'd; for still she made
Scandal her pleasure—and her trade!

A Grand-daughter DAME DOWSON had-
As fair, as fair could be!
Lovely enough to make Men mad;
For, on her cheek's soft downy rose
LOVE seem'd in dimples to repose;
Her clear blue eyes look'd mildly bright
Like ether drops of liquid light,
Or sapphire gems,—which VENUS bore,
When, for the silver-sanded shore,
She left her native Sea!

ANNETTA, was the damsel's name;
A pretty, soft, romantic sound,
Such as a lover's heart may wound;
And set his fancy in a flame:
For had the maid been christen'd JOAN,
Or DEBORAH, or HESTER,—

The little God had coldly prest her,
Or, let her quite alone!
For magic is the silver sound—
Which, often, in a NAME is found!

ANNETTA was belov'd; and She
To WILLIAM gave her vows;
For WILLIAM was as brave a Youth,
As ever claim'd the meed of truth,
And, to reward such constancy,
Nature that meed allows.
But Old DAME DOWSON could not bear
A Youth so brave-a Maid so fair.

The GRANNY GREY, with maxims grave
Oft to ANNETTA lessons gave:
And still the burthen of the Tale
Was, "Keep the wicked Men away,
"For should their wily arts prevail
"You'll surely rue the day!"
And credit was to GRANNY due,
The truth, she, by EXPERIENCE, knew!
ANNETTA blush'd, and promis'd She
Obedient to her will would be.

But Love, with cunning all his own,
Would never let the Maid alone:
And though she dar'd not see her Lover,
Lest GRANNY should the deed discover,
She, for a woman's weapon, still,
From CUPID'S pinion pluck'd a quill:
And, with it, prov'd that human art
Cannot confine the Female Heart.

At length, an assignation She
With WILLIAM slily made,
It was beneath an old Oak Tree,
Whose widely spreading shade
The Moon's soft beams contriv'd to break
For many a Village Lover's sake.
But Envy has a Lynx's eye
And GRANNY DOWSON cautious went
Before, to spoil their merriment,
Thinking no creature nigh.

Young WILLIAM came; but at the tree
The watchful GRANDAM found!
Straight to the Village hasten'd he

And summoning his neighbours round,
The Hedgerow's tangled boughs among,
Conceal'd the list'ning wond'ring throng.
He told them that, for many a night,
An OLD GREY OWL was heard;
A fierce, ill-omen'd, crabbed Bird—
Who fill'd the village with affright.
He swore this Bird was large and keen,
With claws of fire, and eye-balls green;
That nothing rested, where she came;
That many pranks the monster play'd,
And many a timid trembling Maid
She brought to shame
For negligence, that was her own;
Turning the milk to water, clear,
And spilling from the cask, small-beer;
Pinching, like fairies, harmless lasses,
And shewing Imps, in looking-glasses;
Or, with heart-piercing groan,
Along the church-yard path, swift gliding,
Or, on a broomstick, witchlike, riding.
All listen'd trembling; For the Tale
Made cheeks of Oker, chalky pale;
The young a valiant doubt pretended;
The old believ'd, and all attended.

Now to DAME DOWSON he repairs
And in his arms, enfolds the Granny:
Kneels at her feet, and fondly swears
He will be true as any!
Caresses her with well feign'd bliss
And, fearfully, implores a Kiss—
On the green turf distracted lying,
He wastes his ardent breath, in sighing.

The DAME was silent; for the Lover
Would, when she spoke,
She fear'd, discover
Her envious joke:
And she was too much charm'd to be
In haste,—to end the Comedy!

Now WILLIAM, weary of such wooing,
Began, with all his might, hollooing:—
When suddenly from ev'ry bush
The eager throngs impatient rush;
With shouting, and with boist'rous glee
DAME DOWSON they pursue,

And from the broad Oak's canopy,
O'er moonlight fields of sparkling dew,
They bear in triumph the Old DAME,
Bawling, with loud Huzza's, her name;
"A witch, a witch!" the people cry,
"A witch!" the echoing hills reply:

'Till to her home the GRANNY came,
Where, to confirm the tale of shame,
Each rising day they went, in throngs,
With ribbald jests, and sportive songs,
'Till GRANNY of her spleen, repented;
And to young WILLIAM'S ardent pray'r,
To take, for life, ANNETTA fair,—
At last,—CONSENTED.

And should this TALE, fall in the way
Of LOVERS CROSS'D, or GRANNIES GREY,—
Let them confess, 'tis made to prove-
The wisest heads,-TOO WEAK FOR LOVE!

GOLFRE, GOTHIC SWISS TALE

IN FIVE PARTS

Where freezing wastes of dazzl'ing Snow
O'er LEMAN'S Lake rose, tow'ring;
The BARON GOLFRE'S Castle strong
Was seen, the silv'ry peaks among,
With ramparts, darkly low'ring!—

Tall Battlements of flint, uprose,
Long shadowing down the valley,
A grove of sombre Pine, antique,
Amid the white expanse would break,
In many a gloomy alley.

A strong portcullis entrance show'd,
With ivy brown hung over;
And stagnate the green moat was found,
Whene'er the Trav'ller wander'd round,
Or moon-enamour'd Lover.

Within the spacious Courts were seen
A thousand gothic fancies;
Of banners, trophies, armour bright,

Of shields, thick batter'd in the fight,
And interwoven lances.

The BARON GOLFRE long had been
To solitude devoted;
And oft, in pray'r would pass the night
'Till day's vermillion stream of light
Along the blue hill floated.

And yet, his pray'r was little mark'd
With pure and calm devotion;
For oft, upon the pavement bare,
He'd dash his limbs and rend his hair
With terrible emotion!

And sometimes he, at midnight hour
Would howl, like wolves, wide-prowling;
And pale, the lamps would glimmer round-
And deep, the self-mov'd bell would sound
A knell prophetic, tolling!

For, in the Hall, three lamps were seen,
That quiver'd dim;-and near them
A bell rope hung, that from the Tow'r
Three knells would toll, at midnight's hour,
Startl'ing the soul to hear them!

And oft, a dreadful crash was heard,
Shaking the Castle's chambers!
And suddenly, the lights would turn
To paly grey, and dimly burn,
Like faint and dying embers.

Beneath the steep, a Maiden dwelt,
The dove-eyed ZORIETTO;
A damsel blest with ev'ry grace—
And springing from as old a race—
As Lady of LORETTO!

Her dwelling was a Goatherds poor;
Yet she his heart delighted;
Their little hovel open stood,
Beside a lonesome frowning wood.
To travellers—benighted.

Yet oft, at midnight when the Moon
Its dappled course was steering,
The Castle bell would break their sleep,

And ZORIETTO slow would creep—
To bar the wicket—fearing!

What did she fear? O! dreadful thought!
The Moon's wan lustre, streaming;
The dim grey lamps, the crashing sound,
The lonely Bittern—shrieking round
The roof,—with pale light gleaming.

And often, when the wintry wind
Loud whistled o'er their dwelling;
They sat beside their faggot fire
While ZORIETTO'S aged Sire
A dismal Tale was telling.

He told a long and dismal Tale
How a fair LADY perish'd;
How her sweet Baby, doom'd to be
The partner of her destiny
Was by a peasant cherish'd!

He told a long and dismal Tale,
How, from a flinty Tow'r
A Lady wailing sad was seen,
The lofty grated bars between,
At dawnlight's purple hour!

He told a Tale of bitter woe,
His heart with pity swelling,
How the fair LADY pin'd and died,
And how her Ghost, at Christmas-tide—
Would wander,—near her dwelling.

He told her, how a lowly DAME
The LADY, lorn, befriended—
Who chang'd her own dear baby, dead,
And took the LADY'S in its stead—
And then—"Forgive her Heav'n!" He said,
And so, his Story ended.

GOLFRE, PART SECOND

As on the rushy floor she sat,
Her hand her pale cheek pressing;
Oft, on the GOATHERD'S face, her eyes
Would fix intent, her mute surprize—

In frequent starts confessing.

Then, slowly would she turn her head,
And watch the narrow wicket;
And shudder, while the wintry blast
In shrilly cadence swiftly past
Along the neighb'ring thicket.

One night, it was in winter time,
The Castle bell was tolling;
The air was still, the Moon was seen,
Sporting, her starry train between,
The thin clouds round her rolling.

And now she watch'd the wasting lamp,
Her timid bosom panting;
And now, the Crickets faintly sing,
And now she hears the Raven's wing
Sweeping their low roof, slanting.

And, as the wicket latch she clos'd,
A groan was heard!—she trembled!
And now a clashing, steely sound,
In quick vibrations echoed round,
Like murd'rous swords, assembled!

She started back; she look'd around,
The Goatherd Swain was sleeping;
A stagnate paleness mark'd her cheek,
She would have call'd, but could not speak,
While, through the lattice peeping.

And O! how dimly shone the Moon,
Upon the snowy mountain!
And fiercely did the wild blast blow,
And now her tears began to flow,
Fast, as a falling fountain.

And now she heard the Castle bell
Again toll sad and slowly;
She knelt and sigh'd: the lamp burnt pale-
She thought upon the dismal Tale—
And pray'd, with fervour holy!

And now, her little string of beads
She kiss'd,—and cross'd her breast;
It was a simple rosary,
Made of the Mountain Holly-tree,

By Sainted Father's blest!

And now the wicket open flew,
As though a whirlwind fell'd it;
And now a ghastly figure stood
Before the Maiden—while her blood
Congeal'd, as she beheld it!
His face was pale, his eyes were wild,
His beard was dark; and near him
A stream of light was seen to glide,
Marking a poniard, crimson-dyed;
The bravest soul might fear him!

His forehead was all gash'd and gor'd—
His vest was black and flowing
His strong hand grasp'd a dagger keen,
And wild and frantic was his mien,
Dread signs of terror, showing.

"O fly me not!" the BARON cried,
"In HEAV'N'S name, do not fear me!"
Just as he spoke the bell thrice toll'd-
Three paly lamps they now behold-
While a faint voice, cried,—"HEAR ME!"

And now, upon the threshold low,
The wounded GOLFRE, kneeling,
Again to HEAV'N address'd his pray'r;
The waning Moon, with livid glare,
Was down the dark sky stealing.

They led him in, they bath'd his wounds,
Tears, to the red stream adding:
The haughty GOLFRE gaz'd, admir'd!
The Peasant Girl his fancy fir'd,
And set his senses, madding!

He prest her hand; she turn'd away,
Her blushes deeper glowing,
Her cheek still spangled o'er with tears
So the wild rose more fresh appears
When the soft dews are flowing!

Again, the BARON fondly gaz'd;
Poor ZORIETTO trembled;
And GOLFRE watch'd her throbbing breast
Which seem'd, with weighty woes oppress'd,
And softest LOVE, dissembled.

The GOATHERD, fourscore years had seen,
And he was sick and needy;
The BARON wore a SWORD OF GOLD,
Which Poverty might well behold,
With eyes, wide stretch'd, and greedy!

The dawn arose! The yellow light
Around the Alps spread chearing!
The BARON kiss'd the GOATHERD'S child—
"Farewell!" she cried,-and blushing smil'd—
No future peril fearing.

Now GOLFRE homeward bent his way
His breast with passion burning:
The Chapel bell was rung, for pray'r,
And all-save GOLFRE, prostrate there—
Thank'd HEAV'N, for his returning!

GOLFRE. PART THIRD

Three times the orient ray was seen
Above the East cliff mounting,
When GOLFRE sought the Cottage Grace
To share the honours of his race,
With treasures, beyond counting!

The Ev'ning Sun was burning red;
The Twilight veil spread slowly;
While ZORIETTO, near the wood
Where long a little cross had stood,
Was singing Vespers holy.

And now she kiss'd her Holly-beads,
And now she cross'd her breast;
The night-dew fell from ev'ry tree—
It fell upon her rosary,
Like tears of Heav'n twice bless'd!

She knelt upon the brown moss, cold,
She knelt, with eyes, mild beaming!
The day had clos'd, she heard a sigh!
She mark'd the dear and frosty sky
With starry lustre gleaming.

She rose; she heard the draw-bridge chains

Loud clanking down the valley;
She mark'd the yellow torches shine
Between the antique groves of Pine—
Bright'ning each gloomy alley.

And now the breeze began to blow,
Soft-stealing up the mountain;
It seem'd at first a dulcet sound—
Like mingled waters, wand'ring round
Slow falling from a fountain.

And now, in wilder tone it rose,
The white peaks sweeping, shrilly:
It play'd amidst her golden hair
It kiss'd her bosom cold and fair—
And sweet, as vale-born Lily!

She heard the hollow tread of feet
Thridding the piny cluster;
The torches flam'd before the wind-
And many a spark was left behind,
To mock the glow-worm's lustre.

She saw them guard the Cottage door,
Her heart beat high with wonder!
She heard the fierce and Northern blast
As o'er the topmost point it past
Like peals of bursting thunder!

And now she hied her swift along
And reach'd the guarded wicket;
But O! what terror fill'd her soul,
When thrice she heard the deep bell toll—
Above the gloomy thicket.

Now fierce, the BARON darted forth,
His trembling victim seizing;
She felt her blood, in ev'ry vein
Move, with a sense of dead'ning pain,
As though her heart were freezing.

"This night," said he, "Yon castle tow'rs
"Shall echo to their centre!
"For, by the HOLY CROSS, I swear,"—
And straight a CROSS of ruby glare
Did through the wicket enter!

And now a snowy hand was seen

Slow moving, round the chamber
A clasp of pearl, it seem'd to bear—
A clasp of pearl, most rich and rare!
Fix'd to a zone of amber.

And now the lowly Hovel shook,
The wicket open flying,
And by, the croaking RAVEN flew
And, whistling shrill, the night-blast blew
Like shrieks, that mark the dying!

But suddenly the tumult ceas'd—
And silence, still more fearful,
Around the little chamber spread
Such horrors as attend the dead,
Where no Sun glitters chearful!

"Now JESU HEAR ME!" GOLFRE cried,
"HEAR ME," a faint voice mutter'd!
The BARON drew his poniard forth—
The Maiden sunk upon the earth,
And—"Save me Heav'n!" she utter'd.

"Yes, Heav'n will save thee," GOLFRE said,
"Save thee, to be MY bride!"
But while he spoke a beam of light
Shone on her bosom, deathly white,
Then onward seem'd to glide.

And now the GOATHERD, on his knees,
With frantic accent cried,
"O! GOD forbid! that I should see
"The beauteous ZORIETTO, be
"The BARON GOLFRE'S bride!

"Poor Lady! she did shrink and fall,
"As leaves fall in September!
"Then be not BARON GOLFRE'S bride—
"Alack! in yon black tow'r SHE died—
"Full well, I do remember!"

"Oft, to the lattice grate I stole
"To hear her, sweetly singing;
"And oft, whole nights, beside the moat,
"I listen'd to the dying note—
"Till matin's bell was ringing.

"And when she died! Poor Lady dear!

"A sack of gold, she gave,
"That, masses every Christmas day
"Twelve bare-foot Monks should sing, or say,
"Slow moving round her Grave.

"That, at the Holy Virgin's shrine
"Three Lamps should burn for ever—
"That, ev'ry month, the bell should toll,
"For pray'rs to save her Husband's soul—
"I shall forget it, never!"

While thus he spoke, the BARON'S eye
Look'd inward on his soul:
For He the masses ne'er had said—
No lamps, their quiv'ring light had shed,
No bell, been taught to toll!

And yet, the bell did toll, self-mov'd;
And sickly lamps were gleaming;
And oft, their faintly wand'ring light
Illum'd the Chapel aisles at night,
Till MORN'S broad eye, was beaming.

GOLFRE, PART FOURTH

The Maid refus'd the BARON'S suit,
For, well she lov'd another;
The angry GOLFRE'S vengeful rage
Nor pride nor reason could assuage,
Nor pity prompt to smother.

His Sword was gone; the Goatherd Swain
Seem'd guilty, past recalling:
The BARON now his life demands
Where the tall Gibbet skirts the lands
With black'ning bones appalling!

Low at the BARON'S feet, in tears
Fair ZORIETTO kneeling,
The Goatherd's life requir'd;—but found
That Pride can give the deepest wound
Without the pang of feeling.

That Pow'r can mock the suff'rer's woes
And triumph o'er the sighing;
Can scorn the noblest mind oppress'd,

Can fill with thorns the feeling breast
Soft pity's tear denying.

"Take me," she cried, "but spare his age—
"Let me his ransom tender;
"I will the fatal deed atone,
"For crimes that never were my own,
"My breaking heart surrender."

The marriage day was fix'd, the Tow'rs
With banners rich were mounted;
His heart beat high against his side
While GOLFRE, waiting for his bride,
The weary minutes counted.

The snow fell fast, with mingling hail,
The dawn was late, and louring;
Poor ZORIETTO rose aghast!
Unmindful of the Northern blast
And prowling Wolves, devouring.

Swift to the wood of Pines she flew,
Love made the assignation;
For there, the sov'reign of her soul
Watch'd the blue mists of morning roll
Mound her habitation.

The BARON, by a Spy appriz'd,
Was there before his Bride;
He seiz'd the Youth, and madly strew'd
The white Cliff, with his steaming blood,
Then hurl'd him down its side.

And now 'twas said, an hungry wolf
Had made the Youth his prey:
His heart lay frozen on the snow,
And here and there a purple glow
Speckled the pathless way.

The marriage day at length arriv'd,
The Priest bestow'd his blessing:
A clasp of orient pearl fast bound
A zone of amber circling round,
Her slender waist compressing.

On ZORIETTO'S snowy breast
A ruby cross was heaving;
So the pale snow-drop faintly glows,

When shelter'd by the damask rose,
Their beauties interweaving!

And now the holy vow began
Upon her lips to falter!
And now all deathly wan she grew
And now three lamps, of livid hue
Pass'd slowly round the Altar.

And now she saw the clasp of pearl
A ruby lustre taking:
And thrice she heard the Castle bell
Ring out a loud funereal knell
The antique turrets shaking.

O! then how pale the BARON grew,
His eyes wide staring fearful!
While o'er the Virgin's image fair
A sable veil was borne on air
Shading her dim eyes, tearful.

And, on her breast a clasp of pearl
Was stain'd with blood, fast flowing:
And round her lovely waist she wore
An amber zone; a cross she bore

Of rubies—richly glowing.
The Bride, her dove-like eyes to Heav'n
Rais'd, calling Christ to save her!
The cross now danc'd upon her breast;
The shudd'ring Priest his fears confest,
And benedictions gave her.

Upon the pavement sunk the Bride
Cold as a corpse, and fainting!
The pearly clasp, self-bursting, show'd
Her beating side, where crimson glow'd
Three spots, of nature's painting.

Three crimson spots, of deepest hue!
The BARON gaz'd with wonder:
For on his buried Lady's side
Just three such drops had nature dyed,
An equal space asunder.

And now remembrance brought to view,
For Heaven the truth discloses,
The Baby, who had early died,

Bore, tinted on its little side,
Three spots—as red as roses!

Now, ere the wedding-day had past,
Stern GOLFRE, and his Bride
Walk'd forth to taste the ev'ning breeze
Soft sighing, mid the sombre trees,
That drest the mountain's side.

And now, beneath the grove of Pine,
Two lovely Forms were gliding;
A Lady, with a beauteous face!
A Youth with stern, but manly, grace
Smil'd,—as in scorn deriding.

Close, by the wond'ring Bride they pass'd,
The red Sun sinking slowly:
And to the little cross they hied—
And there she saw them, side by side,
Kneeling, with fervour holy.

The little cross was golden ting'd
The western radiance stealing;
And now it bore a purple hue,
And now all black and dim it grew,
And still she saw them, kneeling.

White were their robes as fleecy snow
Their faces pale, yet chearful.
Their golden hair, like waves of light
Shone lust'rous mid the glooms of night;
Their starry eyes were tearful.

And now they look'd to Heav'n, and smil'd,
Three paly lamps descended!
And now their shoulders seem'd to bear
Expanding pinions broad and fair,
And now they wav'd in viewless air!
And so, the Vision ended.

GOLFRE, PART FIFTH

Now, suddenly, a storm arose,
The thunder roar'd, tremendous!
The lightning flash'd, the howling blast
Fierce, strong, and desolating, past

The Altitudes stupendous!

Rent by the wind, a fragment huge
From the steep summit bounded:
That summit, where the Peasant's breast
Found, mid the snow, a grave of rest,
By GOLFRE'S poniard wounded.

Loud shrieks, across the mountain wild,
Fill'd up the pause of thunder:
The groves of Pine the lightning past,
And swift the desolating blast
Scatter'd them wide asunder.

The Castle-turrets seem'd to blaze,
The lightning round them flashing;
The drawbridge now was all on fire,
The moat foam'd high, with furious ire,
Against the black walls dashing.

The Prison Tow'r was silver white,
And radiant as the morning;
Two angels' wings were spreading wide,
The battlements, from side to side—
And lofty roof adorning.

And now the Bride was sore afraid,
She sigh'd, and cross'd her breast;
She kiss'd her simple rosary,
Made of the mountain holly-tree,
By sainted Fathers blest.

She kiss'd it once, she kiss'd it twice;
It seem'd to freeze her breast;
The cold show'rs fell from ev'ry tree,
They fell upon her rosary
Like nature's tears, "twice blest!"

"What do you fear?" the BARON cried—
For ZORIETTO trembled—
"A WOLF," she sigh'd with whisper low,
"Hark how the angry whirlwinds blow
"Like Demons dark assembled.

"That WOLF! which did my Lover slay!"
The BARON wildly started.
"That Wolf accurs'd!" she madly cried—
"Whose fangs, by human gore were died,

"Who dragg'd him down the mountain's side,
"And left me—Broken hearted!"

Now GOLFRE shook in ev'ry joint,
He grasp'd her arm, and mutter'd
Hell seem'd to yawn, on ev'ry side,
"Hear me!" the frantic tyrant cried—
"HEAR ME!" a faint voice utter'd.
"I hear thee! yes, I hear thee well!"

Cried GOLFRE, "I'll content thee.
"I see thy vengeful eye-balls roll—
"Thou com'st to claim my guilty soul—
"The FIENDS—the FIENDS have sent thee!"

And now a Goatherd-Boy was heard—
Swift climbing up the mountain:
A Kid was lost, the fearful hind—
Had rov'd his truant care to find,
By wood-land's side—and fountain.

And now a murm'ring throng advanc'd,
And howlings echoed round them:
Now GOLFRE tried the path to pace,
His feet seem'd rooted to the place,
As though a spell had bound them.

And now loud mingling voices cried—
"Pursue that WOLF, pursue him!"
The guilty BARON, conscience stung,
About his fainting DAUGHTER hung,
As to the ground she drew him.

"Oh! shield me Holy MARY! shield
"A tortur'd wretch!" he mutter'd.
"A murd'rous WOLF! O GOD! I crave
"A dark unhallow'd silent grave—"
Aghast the Caitiff utter'd.

"'Twas I, beneath the GOATHERD'S bed
"The golden sword did cover;
"'Twas I who tore the quiv'ring wound,
"Pluck'd forth the heart, and scatter'd round
"The life stream of thy Lover."

And now he writh'd in ev'ry limb,
And big his heart was swelling;
Fresh peals of thunder echoed strong,

With famish'd WOLVES the peaks among
Their dismal chorus yelling!

"O JESU Save me!" GOLFRE shriek'd-
But GOLFRE shriek'd no more!
The rosy dawn's returning light
Display'd his corse,-a dreadful sight,
Black, wither'd, smear'd with gore!

High on a gibbet, near the wood—
His mangled limbs were hung;
Yet ZORIETTO oft was seen
Prostrate the Chapel aisles between—
When holy mass was sung.

And there, three lamps now dimly burn, —
Twelve Monks their masses saying;
And there, the midnight bell doth toll
For quiet to the murd'rer's soul—
While all around are praying.

For CHARITY and PITY kind,
To gentle souls are given;
And MERCY is the sainted pow'r,
Which beams thro' mis'ry's darkest hour,
And lights the way, —TO HEAVEN!

Mary Robinson – A Short Biography

Mary Robinson was born in Bristol, England on 27th November 1757.

Her father, Nicholas Darby, a naval captain, deserted her mother, Hester, for his mistress when Mary was still a child. With no support from her husband, Hester supported her five children by opening a school for young girls in Little Chelsea, London, (where Mary was teaching by her 14th birthday). On a short return to the family, Captain Darby had the school closed which under English law he was entitled to do.

Mary, who at one point attended a school run by the social reformer and poet Hannah More, came to the attention of actor David Garrick. Acting was to her way into the arts, although in those times it was also a chaotic and difficult time for any actress.

Her mother encouraged Mary to accept a proposal from Thomas Robinson, a clerk who dubiously claimed to have an inheritance, when she was 15. Mary was against this but after being stricken ill, and watching him help nurse both her and her younger brother, she felt that she owed him, and she did not want to disappoint her mother.

After the marriage Mary discovered that her husband had no inheritance, but he did have a taste for living way beyond his means and for several affairs that he made no effort to hide. After her husband squandered their money, the couple fled to Talgarth, Wales where Mary gave birth to a daughter, Mary Elizabeth. Her husband though was now arrested and imprisoned for debt in Fleet Prison. While it was common for prisoners' wives to live with their husbands in debtor's prison children were usually sent to live with relatives and away from the harm of prison. However, Mary was devoted to her daughter and she brought the 6-month-old baby with her into the squalor of the prison.

However, it was here that she discovered she could publish poetry and earn money, as well as be distracted from the harsh reality around her. Mary's poems were popular, especially those published by the Morning Post newspaper.

Additionally, Darby was offered work in copying legal documents in order to pay down his debts. He refused. Mary took the work instead.

'Poems by Mrs. Robinson', was published in 1775 and contained 'twenty-six ballads, odes, and elegies' that 'echo traditional values, praising values such as charity, sincerity, and innocence, particularly in a woman'.

After their release from prison Mary returned to the theatre. Her first performance was playing Juliet, at Drury Lane Theatre in December 1776.

Motivated by the months she spent in prison Mary continued to write and also found a patron in Georgiana Cavendish, Duchess of Devonshire, who sponsored, in 1777, the publication of Mary's 'Captivity, a poem and 'Celadon and Lydia, a Tale'. The collection described the horrors of captivity and painted a sympathetic picture of the 'wretch' and the 'guiltless partners of his poignant woes'.

Her later stage performances as Viola in 'Twelfth Night' and Rosalind in 'As You Like It' won her much praise as also did playing Perdita in 'A Winter's Tale' at 21 in 1779. It was now that she attracted the attention of the young Prince of Wales and the offer of twenty thousand pounds to become his mistress (to be paid when he came of age).

Mary, with her new social status became a trend-setter in London, introducing a loose, flowing muslin gown that became known as the Perdita. But Mary was in a quandary about abandoning her marriage for the Prince as she knew the risk of public opinion and its moralising. During her adult life she struggled to live in the public eye and to stay true to her values. Her desires, and the thought of being treated better, eventually won the day. However, the Prince ended the affair in 1781 and refused to pay the promised sum (although his father, George III, paid her £5000 – enough to buy her creditors off). Mary was back to supporting herself although she did occasionally receive an annuity from the Crown for the return of some letters written by the Prince.

She now lived apart from her husband but engaged in several affairs. It was said at the time that her lover Lord Malden, so sure of her affections, offered a thousand pounds to any man who could seduce her away from him. Banastre Tarleton, a distinguished soldier in the American War of Independence, was that man. Their relationship would last 15 years despite Mary's various illnesses financial problems and the efforts of Tarleton's family to end the relationship.

In 1783, Mary suffered a mysterious illness that left her partially paralysed.

From the late 1780s, Mary's poetry distinguished her so much that she was referred to as 'the English Sappho'. In addition she authored eight novels, three plays, feminist treatises, and an autobiographical manuscript that was incomplete at the time of her death. Mary, striving to separate herself from her past, and life as an actress, took up writing full-time.

She had now also abandoned her Della Cruscan poetic style and instead turned to what she felt was her own voice; 'Poems by Mary Robinson', (1791) and 'Poems by Mrs. Robinson' (1793).

She was undoubtedly a very talented writer. Her friend Samuel Taylor Coleridge called her 'a woman of undoubted genius.' Her 1791 collection had a subscription list of 600 people headed by the Prince of Wales, and other members of the nobility.

In 1792 Mary published her novel 'Vancenza; or The Dangers of Credulity', her most popular work. In 1794 came 'The Widow; or, A Picture of Modern Times' which portrayed themes of manners in the fashionable world.

The satirical poem 'London's Summer Morning', was written in 1795 (but published after her death in 1800). Here Mary described the loud, bustling sounds of the industrialised city. Her characters of chimney-boy, and house-maid described the way English society treated children as both innocent and fragile creatures but also cheap workers.

In 1796, Mary argued for women's equality, their right to education and illustrated ideas of free will, suicide, rationalization, empiricism and relationship to sensibility in 'Sappho and Phæon: In a Series of Legitimate Sonnets'.

In 1796 she wrote 'Angelina; A Novel', but her dwindling audience meant its income was less than its costs.

Although, Mary's novels were not as successful as she hoped, she had a talent for poetry. Mary was praised in literary circles for both her poetry and her prose work. The two best known examples are 'A Letter to the Women of England' (1798) and 'The Natural Daughter' (1799). Both her works deal with the role of women during the Romantic Era. Mary and her contemporary Mary Wollenstonecraft attempted to show how badly women were treated compared to men.

In 1800, after years of declining health and a fall into financial despair, Mary wrote her last piece of literature: 'Lyrical Tales'. The collection gathered works on domestic violence, misogyny, violence against the poor, and political oppression. This last work pleads for a recognition of the moral and rational worth of women: 'Let me ask this plain and rational question,—is not woman a human being, gifted with all the feelings that inhabit the bosom of man?'

Mary Darby Robinson died in poverty at Englefield Cottage, Englefield Green, Surrey, on 26th December 1800, aged 44, having survived several years of ill health.

Mary requested to be buried in Old Windsor church-yard, the sole reason being its close proximity to the place where she and the Prince of Wales had been lovers.

Mary, in her short life, was scandalous, but also educated, and at least partially, independent from her husband. She was an early entrant to successful women writers. She pushed the ideas of equality for women during the late 18th century. Nevertheless, many contemporary women were not taken with how she exposed herself to the public and ostracized her. Her works as an author however continue to enjoy a fine reputation.

Mary Robinson – A Concise Bibliography

Poetry

Poems by Mrs. Robinson (1775)
Captivity, a Poem and Celadon and Lydia, a Tale. Dedicated, by Permission, to Her Grace the Duchess of Devonshire (1777)
Ainsi va le Monde, a Poem. Inscribed to Robert Merry, Esq. A.M. [writing as Laura Maria] (1790)
Poems by Mrs. M. Robinson (1791)
The Beauties of Mrs. Robinson (1791)
Monody to the Memory of Sir Joshua Reynolds, Late President of the Royal Academy, &c. &c. &c. (1792)
Ode to the Harp of the Late Accomplished and Amiable Louisa Hanway (1793)
Modern Manners, a Poem. In Two Cantos. By Horace Juvenal (1793)
Sight, the Cavern of Woe, and Solitude. Poems (1793)
Monody to the Memory of the Late Queen of France (1793)
Poems by Mrs. M. Robinson. Volume the Second (1793)
Poems, by Mrs. Mary Robinson. A New Edition (1795)
Sappho and Phæon. In a Series of Legitimate Sonnets, with Thoughts on Poetical Subjects, and Anecdotes of the Grecian Poetess (1796)
Lyrical Tales, by Mrs. Mary Robinson (1800)
The Mistletoe. A Christmas Tale [Writing as Laura Maria] (1800)

Novels

Vancenza; or, the Dangers of Credulity. In Two Volumes (1792)
The Widow, or a Picture of Modern Times. A Novel, in a Series of Letters, in Two Volumes (1794)
Angelina; a Novel, in Three Volumes (1796)
Hubert de Sevrac, a Romance, of the Eighteenth Century (1796)
Walsingham; or, the Pupil of Nature. A Domestic Story (1797)
The False Friend: A Domestic Story (1799)
Natural Daughter. With Portraits of the Leadenhead Family. A Novel (1799)

Dramas

The Lucky Escape, A Comic Opera (performed on 23 April 1778 at the Theatre Royal, Drury Lane)
The Songs, Chorusses, &c. in The Lucky Escape, a Comic Opera, as Performed at the Theatre-Royal, in Drury-Lane (1778)
Kate of Aberdeen (a comic opera withdrawn in 1793 and never staged)

Nobody. A Comedy in Two Acts (performed on 27 Nov. 1794 at the Theatre Royal, Drury Lane)
The Sicilian Lover. A Tragedy. In Five Acts (1796)

Political Treatises

Impartial Reflections on the Present Situation of the Queen of France; by A Friend to Humanity (1791)
A Letter to the Women of England, on the Injustice of Mental Subordination. With Anecdotes. [Writing as Anne Frances Randall] (1799)
Thoughts on the Condition of Women, and on the Injustice of Mental Subordination (1799)

Essays

The Sylphid. No. I (Morning Post and Gazetteer 29 Oct. 1799)
The Sylphid. No. II (Morning Post and Gazetteer 7 Nov. 1799)
The Sylphid. No. III (Morning Post and Gazetteer 16 Nov. 1799)
The Sylphid. No. IV (Morning Post and Gazetteer 23 Nov. 1799)
The Sylphid. No. V (Morning Post and Gazetteer 27 Nov. 1799)
The Sylphid. No. VI (Morning Post and Gazetteer 7 Dec. 1799)
The Sylphid. No. VII (Morning Post and Gazetteer 19 Dec. 1799)
The Sylphid. No. VIII (Morning Post and Gazetteer 24 Dec. 1799)
The Sylphid. No. IX (Morning Post and Gazetteer 2 Jan. 1800)
To the Sylphid (Morning Post and Gazetteer 4 Jan. 1800)
The Sylphid. No. X (Morning Post and Gazetteer 7 Jan. 1800)
The Sylphid. No. XI (Morning Post and Gazetteer 11 Jan. 1800)
The Sylphid. No. XII (Morning Post and Gazetteer 31 Jan. 1800)
The Sylphid. No. XIII (Memoirs 3: 68-73 no extant copy of Morning Post exists)
Present State of the Manners, Society, &c. of the Metropolis of England (Monthly Magazine Aug. 1800)
Present State of the Manners, Society, &c. of the Metropolis of England (Monthly Magazine Sept. 1800)
Present State of the Manners, Society, &c. of the Metropolis of England (Monthly Magazine Oct. 1800)
Present State of the Manners, Society, &c. of the Metropolis of England (Monthly Magazine Oct. 1800)

Translation

Picture of Palermo by Dr. Hager translated from the German by Mrs. Mary Robinson (1800)

Biographical Sketches

Anecdotes of Eminent Persons: Memoirs of the Late Duc de Biron (Monthly Magazine Feb.1800)
Anecdotes of Eminent Persons: Account of Rev. John Parkhurst (Monthly Magazine July 1800)
Anecdotes of Eminent Persons: Account of Bishop Parkhurst (Monthly Magazine July 1800)
Anecdotes of Eminent Persons: Additional Anecdotes of Philip Egalité Late Duke of Orleans (Monthly Magazine Aug. 1800)
Anecdotes of Eminent Persons: Anecdotes of the Late Queen of France (Monthly Magazine Aug. 1800)

Posthumous Publications

Mr. Robert Ker Porter. Public Characters of 1800-1801 (1801)
Memoirs of the Late Mrs. Robinson, Written by Herself with Some Posthumous Pieces. In Four Volumes (1801)
Jasper. A Fragment, Memoirs of the Late Mrs. Robinson, Volume 3 (1801)
The Poetical Works of the Late Mrs. Mary Robinson: Including Many Pieces Never Before Published. In Three Volumes (1806)
The Savage of Aveyron, Memoirs of the Late Mrs. Robinson, Volume 3 (1801)
The Progress of Liberty, Memoirs of the Late Mrs. Robinson, Volume 4 (1801)

www.ingramcontent.com/pod-product-compliance
Lightning Source LLC
Chambersburg PA
CBHW021937040426
42448CB00008B/1114